P9-CSC-730

ALSO BY JANNA GUR

The Book of New Israeli Food

Jewish Soul Food

Jewish Soul Food

From Minsk to Marrakesh

More Than 100 Unforgettable Dishes
Updated for Today's Kitchen

JANNA GUR

With Nirit Yadin and Ruth Oliver

Photography by Daniel Lailah
Visual Concept and Food Styling by Amit Farber

SCHOCKEN BOOKS   NEW YORK

Copyright © 2014 by Al Hashulchan Gastronomic Media

All rights reserved. Published in the United States by Schocken Books, a division of Random House LLC, New York, and in Canada by Random House of Canada Limited, Toronto, Penguin Random House companies.

Schocken Books and colophon are registered trademarks of Random House LLC.

Library of Congress Cataloging-in-Publication Data
    Gur, Janna
      Jewish Soul Food: From Minsk to Marrakesh, more than 100 unforgettable
    dishes updated for today's kitchen / Janna Gur ; with Nirit Yadin and Ruth Oliver.
         pages   cm
      Includes index.
       ISBN 978-0-8052-4308-6 (hardcover : alk. paper).
       ISBN 978-0-8052-4309-3 (e-book).
      1. Jewish cooking.   I. Yadin, Nirit.   II. Oliver, Ruth (Chef).   III. Title.
    TX724.G873 2014   641.5'676—dc23   2014004467

www.schocken.com

Jacket photograph by Daniel Lailah
Jacket design by Emily Mahon

Printed in China
First Edition

9 8 7 6 5 4 3 2 1

To Ilan

Contents

MEATLESS MAINS

SAVORY PASTRIES

SHABBAT STATE OF MIND

CAKES, COOKIES, AND DESSERTS

Introduction

I was born in Riga, Latvia, and grew up feeling very Jewish yet knowing almost nothing about Judaism—a phenomenon not uncommon among Soviet Jews. The only contact our family had with Jewish tradition was during Passover. My grandparents would go to the only synagogue in town and pick up a couple boxes of matzo that had been shipped to Jewish families "from America." For a few days, I was the most popular girl on the block: Other kids loved these funny Jewish crackers, and I would carefully dole out chunks of matzo in exchange for past or future favors. This privileged position terminated as soon as my supply of matzo ran out.

But I did grow up eating Jewish food—not all the time and not on Jewish holidays, which we never celebrated. In our family, gefilte fish, pickled herring, chopped liver, helzale (stuffed neck), and cholodetz (jellied calf's foot) were party foods, served in cut-glass bowls and on our best china on birthdays, New Year's Eves, and wedding anniversaries. Preparation for these feasts lasted for days on end. I remember watching, transfixed, how my grandma sewed up chicken skin for helzale—the ruby in her ring as deep red as her chipped nail polish. There were also traumatic encounters with the live carp that swam in our bathtub, awaiting their doomsday, when they would be transformed into gefilte fish. As a child, I was a reluctant, picky eater, but I adored all these foods, even the wobbly cholodetz. At the same time, I felt somewhat embarrassed by their obvious Jewishness—the sentiment will be poignantly familiar to those who grew up in the state-endorsed anti-Semitic climate. It was the same kind of uneasiness I felt toward Yiddish, the mother tongue of my grandparents.

In 1974, our family emigrated from Riga to Israel, and I eagerly embarked on a mission of forging a new identity. At the age of fifteen, I wanted nothing more than to look, speak, and eat like a sabra (a nickname for a native Israeli). Connecting to Israeli food was easy—I was quickly seduced by the fresh, spiced tastes of local cooking and dizzying abundance of fruits and vegetables.

In time, through a series of strange turns of fate, I became a food writer and, in 1991, together with my husband, Ilan Gur, founded *Al Hashulchan,* a Hebrew-language food magazine, which I edit to this day. Our timing couldn't have been better: Peace was in the air, the economy was flourishing, and after decades of austerity, Israelis finally felt entitled to embrace the pleasures of good food. Within a few short years, the local food scene exploded with boutique cheese farms, varietal olive oils, artisanal breads, and fine wines. Internationally trained young chefs opened restaurants where they experimented with local ingredients according to the latest culinary vogues.

At *Al Hashulchan,* we felt it was our mission to champion this delicious revolution. In 2008, I authored *The Book of New Israeli Food*—a collection of recipes and stories celebrating Israeli food and the people who create it. Published in Israel and the United States, this book took me on a new journey and made me an unofficial presenter for Israeli gastronomy, and I began speaking at Jewish Community Centers, cooking schools, and synagogues; meeting with the press; and writing articles about local food.

In my lectures and articles I would explain that Israeli cooking draws its inspiration from two major sources: the Middle Eastern cuisines of the countries that surround us and the culinary legacy brought to Israel by Jewish immigrants. The fact that Israel is home to so many communities coming from such far and diverse places—and the interaction between these diverse peoples—is what makes Israeli food so unique. Moroccan, Iraqi, Yemeni, Turkish, and Bulgarian dishes have passed into the culinary mainstream and become all-Israeli favorites. It took me a while to realize that there was a gaping hole in my vision.

"'But what about the memories? Food is not all about recipes and trends. As Israelis, you have a duty to preserve Jewish culture, and food is such an important part of it!'"

My aha moment came one balmy summer evening at a meeting with a group of Canadian food journalists. During a delicious and very nouveau Israeli dinner in a trendy restaurant, one of the journalists remarked that he was surprised to find so little Jewish food in Israel. Of course, by Jewish he meant Ashkenazi; he was referring to the kind of food I grew up eating in Riga. I had my answer ready: "This food is too heavy for our sunny Mediterranean climate, plus it clots your arteries with all that cholesterol. Oh, and don't forget, Moroccan couscous and Iraqi kubbe are as Jewish as gefilte fish." He looked disappointed. "But what about the memories? Food is not all about recipes and trends. As Israelis, you have a duty to preserve Jewish culture, and food is such an important part of it!"

Oddly, I had never thought about it that way. I was so involved in celebrating our brave *new* culinary world that I regarded Jewish cuisines as a means to an end— a playing field for Israeli chefs, fertile ground on which the nascent Israeli cuisine could thrive. Though fascinated by its variety and history, I had judged Jewish cooking mainly by its relevance to contemporary cooking in general, and to Israeli cooking in particular. At this point, I started to look at it with new eyes and embarked on a new journey, one that looks back rather than forward. With that came a realization that this journey is actually a race against time, and that the time is quite short.

Wherever Jews settled in the Diaspora, they created cuisines. They had to. Naturally, they were influenced by the ingredients and cooking styles of the countries in which they lived, but their kitchens were also different from the kitchens of their neighbors. Kosher dietary laws precluded their using certain foods and combinations; even more important, these laws, which progressively became more strict and all-encompassing, imposed on them a degree of culinary isolation: Jews not only cooked and ate differently, they were not allowed to sample the nonkosher food of the Gentiles. A few years ago, I watched a television interview with a Yemenite Jew who had recently arrived in Israel. When he was asked whether his food tasted different from that of his Muslim neighbors, he looked puzzled: "How would I know? I have never tried it."

The concept of kashruth made Jewish food different. It also made it extremely significant: To a large extent Jews are defined (in their own eyes and in the eyes of the others) by what they eat and don't eat. The centrality of cooking in Jewish culture is especially evident on Shabbat and holidays. Shabbat poses an almost impossible challenge: The day on which even the poorest must eat a proper meal is also the day on which no fire can be lit and no manual work can be done. And the result: Across the globe, unique dishes were devised for Friday-night dinners and Shabbat lunches. Holiday cooking is where Jewish cuisines are at their most exuberant. At the core of almost every holiday, there is a festive, elaborate meal—from the strictly regulated ceremonial menu served at a Passover Seder to the symbolic foods consumed at Rosh Hashanah.

Last but not least, Jewish cuisines are unique because they reflect the histories of their respective communities. Many Eastern European Ashkenazi dishes preserve archaic influences from Alsace and even Italy; the cooking of Turkish and Bulgarian Jews bears similarities to that of their ancestors during the Golden Age in Spain; the cuisines of Iraqi Jews and Indian Jews have a lot in common because of close ties between these communities.

This world of culinary wisdom faced dramatic changes in the twentieth century as the vast majority of those scattered in the Jewish Diaspora ceased (or nearly ceased) to exist in their original provenances. Millions of Jews from all over the world immigrated to Israel, a tiny country with an ambition to reinvent itself as a nation. The culinary baggage Jewish repatriates brought with them was at first a burden rather than a legacy. In the early days of the Zionist movement, there was an overwhelming impulse to reject the Diaspora—its customs, its language, its foods.

Later on, as waves of immigrants flooded the country in the wake of World War II, the ideological rejection was replaced by something more poignant: children ashamed of the immigrant ways of their parents—their language, their customs, their food. Be it an Ashkenazi boy embarrassed in front of his classmates because of his chopped liver sandwich or a Moroccan girl who wouldn't let her mother serve North African sweets at her birthday party. The parents, on the other hand, clung tenaciously to their culinary legacy as a way to preserve their identities—to connect with their families, to remember their homes.

"Can these cuisines, which are products of the unique circumstances of Jewish life in places like Iraq, Turkey, Yemen, Morocco, or Poland, really survive in their new home? Or to put it in simpler words: Who will cook this food in the next generation and who will eat it?"

Toward the end of the millennium, as the ethos of the melting pot gave way to more inclusive approaches to everything cultural, the foods of Jewish communities became again a source of pride and inspiration, even for a younger generation, certainly for Israeli chefs. Some cuisines did better than others: Balkan and North African food traditions that suit the local climate and ingredients so well are among the most beloved in modern-day Israel. Ashkenazi food, which in the eyes of the world is synonymous with "Jewish cooking," is less popular, but recent years have brought a new interest in it, sparked by the trendiness of Jewish Ashkenazi cooking in North America, especially in New York.

Today, more and more Israelis are aware of the importance of preserving their family cooking heritages. Self-published family cookbooks have become very common, and it is touching to see how much love and longing are invested in these modest publications. Still the big question looms: Can these cuisines, which are products of the unique circumstances of Jewish life in places like Iraq, Turkey, Yemen, Morocco, or Poland, really survive in their new home? Or to put it in simpler words: Who will cook this food in the next generation and who will eat it? Much of it is a labor-intensive, time-consuming, old-fashioned kind of cooking. Indeed, in most families it is the grandmother who still cooks the food from the old country. Her children, long since busy parents themselves, love it, but don't have time to cook it. As for the grandchildren, they probably have tasted it only at a few family occasions, and by the time they are old enough to care and get interested, the grandmother is gone, and when they ask the mother how to make something, she often doesn't know. "I should have asked her for the recipe but never got around to it and now it is too late." You have no idea how often I have heard this!

Gastronomy may seem to lend itself easily to preservation, especially in our digital age. But transcribing a recipe or even videoing it is not nearly enough. The only way to really preserve a culinary culture—to keep it alive—is to cook the food and make people want to eat it. It would be naive to assume that all the wealth of Jewish cooking can be kept alive in this way. Most of it eventually will be relegated to the folkloristic fringes of the culinary scene. But in the world of Jewish food, there are so many dishes that are delicious, exciting, and doable that they can survive relocation and gain a new lease on life in the modern kitchen.

It is with these thoughts that I approached the project that eventually became this book. The Jewish bookshelf is brimming with excellent works. Some of them are encyclopedic in their scope; others, dedicated to the cooking of a specific community, offer a captivating blend of recipes, folklore, and history. But this depth and scope can sometimes be overwhelming, especially to someone new in the field. I felt that what was missing was something more focused, edited, and therefore approachable; I decided to confine myself to about one hundred dishes from as many Jewish communities as possible—a kind of greatest hits from our Jewish grandmothers.

In selecting the dishes, I tried to crack the code of a winning dish—what is it that makes us adopt and adapt a certain recipe and abandon another? Surely, there's the relative ease of preparation, and the availability of ingredients, but there's something else—the "soul" of a dish, that elusive quality that makes us relish it and want to make it ours. To discover that soul was my goal, but I cannot really claim that it was just I who curated this selection.

Israel today is a living laboratory of Jewish food, as our cooks, both professional and amateur, are exposed to a multitude of cuisines and dishes. Through a process of natural selection, some of them have been discovered and adopted by the whole society because of their deliciousness and practicality. In this respect, the real editors of this collection are anonymous Israelis who prepare these dishes in their kitchens or order them in restaurants, and in this way are keeping them alive.

"What is it that makes us adopt and adapt a certain recipe and abandon another? Surely, there's the relative ease of preparation, and the availability of ingredients, but there's something else—the 'soul' of a dish, that elusive quality that makes us relish it and want to make it ours."

I was also very lucky: During the twenty-odd years of editing an Israeli food magazine, I learned from many great cooks around me and was able to compare different versions of the same dish. Many recipes in this book are indeed credited to specific cooks—professional and amateur—while others are the sum total of tips and techniques I picked up along the way.

Most recipes are authentic (often with little tweaks that make life easier), but here and there I was tempted to offer a creative take on a traditional dish: like Erez Komarovsky's Gondalach—a charming fusion of Ashenazi kneidlach and Persian gondi dumplings; or Omer Miller's Exiles Cholent, which cleverly blends ingredients and techniques from several Shabbat casseroles with delicious results.

It was important for me to show that these dishes feel perfectly at home in a modern kitchen (they certainly do in mine): The salads and snacks featured in the first chapter are great for parties and cookouts; Meatless Mains offers healthful and nutritious options for both weekday and special-occasion meals. The Shabbat chapter might lead you to rethink your weekend menu and invite friends for "Sabich breakfast" or serve them a visually stunning and easy-to-make Hamin Macaroni.

As these recipes come from so many different cuisines, some of the ingredients might be a little hard to come by. Wherever possible, more readily available substitutes are suggested, but I do urge you to try to get the real stuff at least once—the difference can be dramatic.

To use a culinary metaphor, I would like to regard this selection as an appetizer—a sampler that will encourage you to explore more dishes from various Jewish cuisines. If you enjoy Lakhoukh panfried bread, you might be tempted to look further afield and discover other distinctive breads from the Yemenite kitchen; while T'bit—an ingenious Iraqi Shabbat casserole—could be a wonderful introduction to one of the most ancient and unique Jewish cuisines. I can also envision a different scenario—your encountering a dish that you remember from your childhood and deciding, for the first time in your life, to make it in your own kitchen.

Either way, every dish you cook from this book (or other Jewish cookbooks for that matter) is meaningful in a way that goes beyond its taste and your personal enjoyment. By cooking it and serving it to those you love, you help to keep it alive and pass it on to the next generation.

Starters, Salads, and Noshes

They call them meze in the Middle East, zakuski in Russia, and in Israel they are collectively known as salatim ("salads")—small plates of raw and cooked treats, mainly vegetables but some with meat and fish. Flavors and ingredients vary widely, but the concept remains. When I entertain, I love starting the meal with this colorful array of dishes and often find that after such a feast, a main course is quite redundant. I also love, in a very Israeli fashion, to mix foods from various origins: Ashkenazi chopped liver feels right at home next to the smoky flavors of North African mashawia salad, and the lemony Sephardic apio is a lovely garnish for Aleppan meat and herb latkes.

SPICY CARROT SALAD

MOROCCAN

To make this simple and tasty meze salad you will need two typical North African condiments—pickled lemons and harissa. Both can be made at home or bought at specialty food stores or Middle Eastern groceries, and both will prove useful and versatile additions to your pantry.

Serves 6 to 8

6 medium carrots, sliced into ¾-inch (2-cm) coins

3 cups water

1½ teaspoons sugar

1½ teaspoons salt

3 tablespoons fresh lemon juice

1 to 2 tablespoons harissa (page 7 or store-bought)

1 tablespoon pickled (Moroccan) lemons, finely chopped (see below or store-bought)

5 garlic cloves, minced

3 tablespoons fresh lemon juice

1 teaspoon ground cumin

¼ cup extra virgin olive oil

Salt

¼ cup fresh cilantro or mint leaves, chopped

1. Put the sliced carrots in a saucepan and add the water, sugar, salt, and lemon juice. Bring to a boil, reduce the heat, and simmer, partially covered, for 10 to 12 minutes, until the carrots are tender but still have some bite.

2. Transfer the carrots to a bowl (save some of the cooking liquid). Add the harissa, pickled lemons, garlic, lemon juice, cumin, olive oil, salt, and about ¼ cup of the cooking liquid and mix. Let cool. Taste and adjust the seasoning.

3. Refrigerate for a few hours, preferably overnight, to let the flavors meld. The salad will keep for 3 to 4 days in the fridge. Before serving, bring to room temperature and toss with the cilantro.

Pickled Lemons | MOROCCAN

For me, pickled lemons define the concept of a "secret ingredient." Less sharp than fresh lemons; soft, aromatic, and spicy, they perform miracles in vegetable and grain salads and are a great addition to chicken and fish braises. I also use them in pasta sauces, especially those with tuna. Preparation is easy, but the curing process takes about three months.

Makes 2 pounds/1 kg

2 pounds (1 kg) lemons, thinly sliced or cut into small wedges, pips removed

1 cup coarse salt

5 garlic cloves

2 small hot chile peppers (red or green)

4 to 6 allspice berries

4 bay leaves

Sweet and/or hot paprika

Fresh lemon juice, to cover

Vegetable oil, to seal

1. Dip the lemon slices or wedges in the salt to cover all sides and arrange in layers in a sterilized glass jar. Place the garlic, chiles, allspice, and bay leaves between the layers of lemon. Press down hard until the juice begins to run out and pour the lemon juice on top. To seal, pour a generous layer of vegetable oil on top of everything.

2. Refrigerate for 3 weeks and up to a month. When the curing process has been completed, discard the garlic, chiles, allspice, and bay leaves and keep refrigerated.

BEET SALAD WITH CUMIN AND CINNAMON

MOROCCAN

A close relative of Spicy Carrot Salad (page 2), this one is even easier to prepare. The original recipe calls for boiling the beets, but roasting them on a bed of coarse salt will release earthy flavors that blend beautifully with the spices and the herbs. Don't worry—once you peel them, the beets won't be salty at all, just less watery (salt absorbs liquids) and bursting with flavor.

Serves 6 to 8

1 pound (½ kg) coarse salt

4 large or 6 medium beets, unpeeled

½ teaspoon ground cumin

½ teaspoon ground cinnamon

⅓ cup fresh lemon juice

2 tablespoons extra virgin olive oil

Salt and freshly ground black pepper

3 tablespoons chopped fresh parsley

1. Preheat the oven to 400°F (200°C). Line a baking sheet with parchment and spread the salt in an even layer.

2. Arrange the beets on the bed of salt and roast until they look shrunken and are fork tender, about 1 hour.

3. Cool the beets slightly and peel (use gloves to prevent your hands and nails from turning purple). Cut into wedges or large cubes.

4. Transfer the beets to a bowl and add the cumin, cinnamon, lemon juice, olive oil, salt, and pepper. Taste and adjust the seasoning.

5. Refrigerate for a few hours, preferably overnight, to blend the flavors. The salad will keep for 3 to 4 days in the fridge. Before serving, bring to room temperature and toss with the parsley.

ORANGE AND BLACK OLIVES SALAD

MOROCCAN

When tangy-sweet oranges meet the sharp saltiness of olives, something magical happens. Yet another enticing salad from the Moroccan meze table.

Serves 6

2 ounces (50 g) black oil-cured olives, pitted and halved

4 to 5 oranges, peeled, quartered, and coarsely sliced

1 tablespoon harissa (see below or store-bought)

1 tablespoon fresh cilantro leaves, chopped

½ teaspoon ground cumin

⅓ cup fresh lemon juice

3 tablespoons extra virgin olive oil

3 to 4 garlic cloves, chopped

Mix the olives, oranges, harissa, cilantro, cumin, lemon juice, olive oil, and garlic and let stand for at least 3 hours to blend the flavors. Serve at room temperature. The salad will keep for 2 days in the fridge.

Harissa | NORTH AFRICAN

What I like about harissa, besides the taste of dried red peppers, is the fact that it is not overly spicy, so you can use it quite liberally and even serve it on the table as a condiment.

Makes 2 cups

1 pound (½ kg) dried sweet red chile peppers

2 to 3 dried hot red chile peppers

10 garlic cloves

½ cup extra virgin olive oil

1 tablespoon salt

1 tablespoon ground cumin

Juice of 2 lemons

1. Grind the dried chiles and the garlic in a mortar and pestle or in a meat grinder. A blender may be used as well, but it will produce a more liquid harissa. Transfer to a bowl.

2. Stir in the olive oil, salt, cumin, and lemon juice. Taste and adjust the seasoning. It will last a long time in a tightly covered container in the refrigerator.

BLUE ONES WITH RED ONES | Eggplant Salad with Tomatoes and Onions

ROMANIAN

My maternal grandparents, Rosa and Usher, hail from Kishinev, the capital of Bessarabia (a province of Romania). After World War II, they moved to Riga, Latvia, but in all matters culinary, they remained true Bessarabians. Once a year a suitcase full of fresh eggplants would arrive with a relative from their hometown (no one cooked eggplants in Riga), and Rosa would cook up a storm. She would then call Vera, my other grandmother and her culinary archrival, to say, "Come by, Veruchka, I cooked blue ones [that is, eggplants] with red ones [that is, tomatoes]." "And so I went," Vera told her friends over a cup of coffee with cream, her voice thick with irony. "But forget the blue ones and the red ones; she just served us some grayish goo. . . . " That "grayish goo" was the best eggplant salad I have ever tasted. To get the authentic flavor, try to find unrefined sunflower oil (available in Russian grocery stores or online; see Mail Order Sources, page 203). Its strong nutty aroma adds a lot of character to the salad. Otherwise, use fruity extra virgin olive oil.

Serves 4 to 6

2 large or 3 medium eggplants

2 large ripe tomatoes, plus 1 sliced, for garnish

2 onions

1 to 2 garlic cloves, crushed (optional)

Juice from ½ lemon

⅓ cup unrefined sunflower oil or fruity extra virgin olive oil

Salt and freshly ground black pepper

1. Place the eggplants on a rack over the open flame of the stove. Roast, turning occasionally, until the skins are charred and the flesh feels soft. The eggplants can also be roasted in a hot oven (450°F/250°C) under a broiler or grilled over hot charcoals. Cool slightly, to avoid burning your hands.

2. Peel the eggplants, taking care to remove all bits of charred skin, or cut in half lengthwise and scoop out the flesh. Transfer the flesh to a colander to drain, for an hour. Chop the flesh coarsely and transfer to a bowl.

3. Grate 1 tomato (see page 162) and coarsely chop 1 tomato.

4. Grate 1 onion on a coarse grater and squeeze out the excess liquid. Chop the other one.

5. Add the grated and chopped tomatoes, the onions, and garlic (if using). Add the lemon juice, sunflower oil, salt, and pepper and mix thoroughly. Taste and adjust the seasoning.

6. Garnish with tomato slices and serve at room temperature. The salad will keep in the fridge for 2 to 3 days.

MATBOUKHA | Pepper and Tomato Slow-Cooked Salsa

NORTH AFRICAN

In North African homes, matboukha (meaning "cooked" in Arabic) is part of a meze table, but this spicy, juicy concoction is so much more. It makes a wonderful base for other North African dishes, such as Shakshuka (page 103), spicy meatballs, or fish tagine. I even use it as pasta sauce. If tomatoes are in season, go for fresh, ripe ones. Off-season, canned tomatoes work better (see the variation). Preparation is pretty straightforward, but lengthy, and you will have to stick around and check the pot every now and then to make sure your matboukha doesn't burn or dry out. Therefore, if you are going to make the effort, cook a large pot of matboukha and freeze it in small containers.

Makes about 1 quart / 1 liter

3 red bell peppers

1 fresh hot chile pepper
(red or green)

6½ pounds (3 kg) ripe tomatoes

8 garlic cloves

¼ cup olive oil, plus more to finish the dish

1 tablespoon sweet paprika

1 teaspoon ground cumin (optional)

½ tablespoon sugar

Salt and freshly ground black pepper

1. Roast the bell peppers and chile over an open flame or under the broiler until the skins are charred. Transfer to a plastic container and close. Allow to cool (the peppers' skin will separate from the flesh). Peel and remove the seeds and membranes. Cut into strips. Set aside.

2. Bring a large pot of salted water to a boil and prepare a bowl of ice water large enough to contain the tomatoes. Make a small crisscross on top of each tomato and blanch the tomatoes for 1 to 2 minutes. Transfer to the ice water until cool enough to handle. Peel, halve, remove the seeds, and chop coarsely.

3. Put the roasted peppers, tomatoes, garlic, olive oil, paprika, cumin (if using), sugar, salt, and pepper in a heavy-bottomed pot, preferably nonstick. Cover and cook over very low heat for 2 hours, stirring occasionally, until reduced by half, thick, and shiny. If the mixture becomes too dry, add a little water (2 to 3 tablespoons at a time).

4. Taste and adjust the seasoning; the flavors should be balanced and quite spicy. Remove from the heat and allow to cool. Pour into plastic or glass containers. Drizzle olive oil over and transfer to the refrigerator or freezer. Serve at room temperature.

VARIATION

If fresh summer tomatoes are unavailable, substitute five or six 28-ounce (½ L) cans of peeled whole tomatoes. Drain them but reserve the liquid. Chop roughly and cook with about 1 cup of the liquid. For a brighter taste, add 2 to 3 fresh tomatoes, peeled and seeded.

MASHAWIA | Fresh Tomatoes and Roasted Peppers Salsa

NORTH AFRICAN

This salad is like an uncooked version of Matboukha (page 9). Because the tomatoes used are fresh, mashawia is worth making only when they are in season. Canned tomatoes just wouldn't do and neither would bland-tasting hothouse ones. With its bold flavors and vibrant colors, mashawia is a perfect companion for grilled meats or a plate of hummus and a tasty addition to the meze table.

Serves 4 to 6

4 red bell peppers

1 hot green chile pepper, thinly sliced

4 ripe, juicy sweet summer tomatoes

1 onion, diced

½ cup chopped fresh parsley

¼ cup chopped fresh cilantro (optional)

3 tablespoons olive oil

2 tablespoons fresh lemon juice

Salt

I. Roast the bell peppers and chile over an open flame or under the broiler until the skins are charred. Transfer to a plastic container and close. Allow to cool (the peppers' skin will separate from the flesh). Peel, remove the seeds and membranes, and roughly chop. Set aside.

2. Bring a large pot of salted water to a boil and prepare a bowl of ice water large enough to contain the tomatoes. Make a small crisscross on top of each tomato and blanch the tomatoes for 1 to 2 minutes. Transfer to the ice water until cool enough to handle. Peel, halve, remove the seeds, and chop coarsely. Set aside.

3. Combine the roasted peppers, tomatoes, onion, parsley, and cilantro (if using) in a large bowl. Season with the olive oil, lemon juice, and salt and mix thoroughly. Taste and adjust the seasoning.

4. Transfer to a sealed container and store in the refrigerator for up to 3 days. Serve at room temperature.

VARIATIONS

• Instead of blanching the tomatoes, roast them over an open flame or under the broiler along with the bell peppers and chile. Cool in a sealed container, peel, remove the seeds, and chop as described. The salad will have a softer texture and a more pronounced smoky flavor.

• Add the chopped flesh of 1 to 2 roasted eggplants (see the Romanian eggplant salad on page 8 for instructions on roasting eggplants) to the salad. The result will be similar to another famous North African salad called za'alouk.

GEHAKTE LEBER | Chopped Liver with Lots and Lots of Fried Onions

ASHKENAZI

This beloved Jewish delicacy has countless variants. A big fan of chopped liver, I have tried many and found this to be one of the best. Created by the talented chef Omer Miller, it has twice as much onion in it as liver. And indeed the onion, fried to sweetness, adds a wonderful flavor and soft texture.

Unless you are lucky enough to live in the vicinity of an old-world butcher shop, you will likely have to order chicken livers in advance. Ask the butcher to throw in some goose or chicken fat to make schmaltz (page 14), and also to clean the livers for you.

Serves 6 to 8

⅓ cup schmaltz (see page 14) or vegetable oil

2 pounds (1 kg) onions, coarsely chopped

1 pound (½ kg) fresh chicken livers, thoroughly cleaned (ask the butcher to clean them for you)

Salt and freshly ground black pepper

6 hard-boiled eggs

For the topping (optional)

¼ cup schmaltz (see page 14) or vegetable oil

2 onions, halved and thinly sliced

1. Heat the schmaltz in a large heavy-bottomed frying pan over low heat. Add the onions and sauté slowly for about 20 minutes, until very soft and browned. The onions should be caramelized but not burned. Remove the onions with a slotted spoon, place in a bowl, and set aside.

2. Sauté the livers in the same frying pan for 5 to 6 minutes, turning occasionally until they are browned on both sides. Season generously with salt and pepper and allow to cool. Remove the livers to the bowl with the onions. Cover the livers and onions with plastic wrap and store in the refrigerator for a few hours or, preferably, overnight.

3. Put the livers and onions and the hard-boiled eggs in a food processor and pulse until you reach the desired consistency. It should be quite smooth but still have some texture. If you prefer a chunkier texture, chop finely with a knife. Season with additional salt and pepper.

4. **Prepare the topping** Heat the schmaltz in a medium frying pan. Add the onions and fry over medium heat for 15 minutes until deeply browned and crispy. Set on a paper towel to absorb the excess schmaltz.

5. Sprinkle over the chopped livers before serving.

SCHMALTZ AND GRIBENES

Schmaltz, rendered chicken or goose fat, had been the secret ingredient of Ashkenazi cooks until its fall from grace during the fat-phobia era. Food writer Nirit Yadin tracked down the flavor she remembered from her grandmother, who grew up in a small Jewish shtetl in the Ukraine.

My grandmother was a career woman who avoided the kitchen as much as she could. But on Fridays she would step in, complain profusely, and produce excellent Ashkenazi food. She used schmaltz in everything—in chopped liver, in egg salad, in matzo balls, and, best of all, she would let us dip our challah in schmaltz (it's liquid at room temperature) and eat it with a crunchy, spicy homemade pickle.

One Shabbat in the 1970s, we gathered as usual for Shabbat lunch, but the schmaltz was gone. That was the first time in my life I'd heard the word "cholesterol." Grandma introduced us to the substitute: chopped onions simmered in oil until caramelized. They had their own charm, but they weren't schmaltz.

Thirty years later, fat made its comeback and I reconnected with my grandmother's forgotten wonder. Only then did I discover its by-product gribenes, addictive bits of crunchy onions and chicken cracklings. How come I'd never had those before? My guess is that my grandparents ate them all by themselves.

Makes I pound (½ kg)

1 pound (½ kg) chicken skin and fat, rinsed and diced

1 large onion, halved and thinly sliced

1. Heat the skin and fat over low heat, stirring and breaking up the skin with a rubber spatula.

2. When the fat starts to melt and get slightly brown, add the onion and continue cooking until the onion and cracklings are golden brown and crunchy. Be careful not to burn the fat.

3. Let cool slightly and strain through a sieve into a bowl, making sure that the fat is free of onion and cracklings. Pour the fat (now it's schmaltz) into a glass jar, cover, and refrigerate. The schmaltz will keep for a few months in the refrigerator.

4. Store the onions and cracklings (now they are gribenes) in a separate glass container, cover, and refrigerate. They will keep in the refrigerator for 3 to 4 days. Heat to crisp them up before eating. Use wherever you would use crispy fried onions.

Note | Nirit uses only organic chickens. They tend to have less fat, but fat is where the body stores unwanted chemicals and toxins.

EREZ'S CHOPPED LIVER

I n this unorthodox take on chopped liver, Erez Komarovsky (my favorite Israeli chef) replaces fried onions with oodles of slowly sautéed leeks. He then coats the livers with a spice crust, roasts them, and chops them. Irresistible!

Serves 12

¾ cup fruity olive oil

5 to 6 large leeks (white and light green parts), thinly sliced

1½ tablespoons white peppercorns

1½ tablespoons green peppercorns

1 teaspoon cumin seeds

1 teaspoon mustard seeds

2 pounds (1 kg) fresh chicken livers, thoroughly cleaned (ask the butcher to clean them for you)

Coarse sea salt

1. Heat ½ cup of the olive oil in a frying pan. Add the leeks and sauté over low heat for 20 minutes, stirring occasionally, until they are very soft. Make sure they don't brown. Set aside.

2. Crush the white peppercorns, green peppercorns, cumin seeds, and mustard seeds in a mortar and pestle or in a clean coffee or spice grinder.

3. Brush the livers with a little oil and coat them with the spices and the salt.

4. Thoroughly heat a heavy cast-iron skillet and roast the livers for 5 to 6 minutes, until they are browned. Cool slightly.

5. Chop the livers with a large heavy knife, mix with the leeks, and serve promptly.

ZIBALE MIT EYER | Egg and Onion Salad

ASHKENAZI

The typical chunky texture of this hearty appetizer is obtained by coarsely grinding the ingredients. Tradition calls for a meat grinder (like the one in the photograph), which you probably don't have in your kitchen. Instead, you can briefly pulse the ingredients in a food processor or, better still, chop them with a large sharp knife. Serve with thick slices of rye bread, challah, or bagels.

Serves 4

2 tablespoons schmaltz
(see page 14), butter, or vegetable oil
2 onions, thinly sliced
4 hard-boiled eggs
2 tablespoons mayonnaise
1½ teaspoons whole grain mustard
Salt and freshly ground black pepper

1. Heat the schmaltz in a saucepan over low heat. Add the onions and sauté, stirring occasionally, for 10 to 15 minutes, until the onions are very soft and golden brown. Remove from the heat.

2. Grind the sautéed onions and hard-boiled eggs in a meat grinder or pulse in a food processor to create a uniformly chunky paste (be careful not to puree them). Alternatively, coarsely chop the onions with a knife and grate the eggs on a coarse grater. Transfer to a bowl.

3. Stir in the mayonnaise and mustard and season with salt and pepper. The salad tastes best when eaten immediately, but you can also keep it, covered, in the refrigerator for up to 3 days.

VARIATION

Before serving, add 2 to 3 tablespoons finely chopped scallions or chives to the salad. They will add zest and a pretty green color.

BADRIJANI NIGVZIT | Eggplant Rolls with Walnut and Herb Filling

GEORGIAN

These look like Italian involtini, but the filling is unique and typically Georgian: pureed walnuts perfumed with fresh herbs (parsley and cilantro), garlic, and vinegar. When pomegranates are in season, add fresh pomegranate seeds for crunch and flavor. I got this recipe from Marina Toporiya, a Georgian cook who used to own a modest restaurant in downtown Tel Aviv, where she turned out wonderful and unusual dishes from the old country.

Makes 12 to 14 rolls

For the eggplants

Unbleached all-purpose flour, for dredging

Salt

Vegetable oil for frying

2 to 3 eggplants, very thinly sliced lengthwise (you should have about 14 long, thin slices)

For the filling

12 ounces (350 g) walnuts

2 garlic cloves, crushed

1 onion, roughly chopped

1 teaspoon (or less) cayenne pepper

½ teaspoon ground turmeric

¼ teaspoon crushed red pepper flakes

½ teaspoon sweet paprika

½ cup chopped fresh parsley

½ cup chopped fresh cilantro

¼ cup white wine vinegar

2 tablespoons water

Salt

Seeds from ½ pomegranate (optional)

1. Prepare the eggplants Put some flour in a shallow bowl and season with salt.

2. Heat a frying pan over medium heat and coat with a ½-inch (1½-cm) layer of vegetable oil. Dip each slice of eggplant into the flour mixture, then put in the pan, being careful not to crowd the pan (work in batches, if necessary). Fry the slices for about 2 minutes per side, until lightly browned. Transfer to a paper towel–lined plate and allow to cool.

3. Prepare the filling Put the walnuts, garlic, onion, cayenne, turmeric, red pepper flakes, paprika, parsley, cilantro, vinegar, water, and salt in a food processor and puree until smooth. Transfer to a bowl and stir in the pomegranate seeds (if using).

4. Spread a heaping spoonful of the filling on a fried eggplant slice and roll up the slice tightly. Place, seam-side down, on a plate and continue with the remaining filling and eggplants. Serve promptly.

TIP

Certain eggplants, especially those with lots of seeds, tend to be bitter. To get rid of the bitterness, sprinkle the sliced eggplants with coarse salt and set in a colander for an hour. Wash, pat dry with paper towels, and fry as directed.

KUKU SABZI | Herb Frittata

PERSIAN

Fresh herbs are essential in Persian cooking and are used in abundance in various dishes (for example, Ghormeh Sabzi, page 99, or the green Persian rice on page 110). Here they form the basis for a fluffy, brightly green egg preparation, which can be enjoyed hot, straight from the pan, or cold—stuffed into pita, along with tahini and pickles. The recipe calls for a combination of spinach, parsley, and dill, but feel free to vary the herbs according to your personal preference or their availability.

Serves 4 to 6

5 to 6 eggs

2 scant tablespoons unbleached all-purpose flour

8 to 10 scallions (white and green parts)

1 packed cup spinach leaves

1 bunch fresh parsley

1 bunch fresh dill

1 teaspoon salt

1 teaspoon freshly ground black pepper

2 tablespoons pine nuts, toasted

1 to 2 tablespoons olive oil

1. Put the eggs, flour, scallions, spinach, parsley, and dill in a food processor. Pulse until the herbs are chopped. Transfer to a bowl, season with salt and pepper, and stir in the pine nuts.

2. Heat the olive oil in a nonstick sauté pan and pour in the egg mixture. Turn the flame to high for a minute, then reduce the heat to medium-low and cook, covered, for 4 to 6 minutes.

3. Remove the lid and check that the eggs are fully set. Carefully flip the entire frittata and fry for another 30 seconds. Remove from the heat, cut into wedges, and serve on a plate or in a pita. It is also excellent cold.

TIP

Instead of flipping the frittata (a procedure that usually ends up with most of the egg mixture splattered all over the stove top), use an ovenproof pan, and once the eggs are set, transfer the pan to a hot oven (400°F/200°C) and broil for a couple minutes until the top is golden. When I prepare kuku sabzi this way, I am often tempted to grate some cheese on top (Parmesan, mozzarella, or pecorino) before I transfer it to the oven. Not authentic in the least, but yummy.

IJEH B'LAHMEH | Herb and Meat Latkes

SYRIAN

A relative of Kuku Sabzi (page 21), ijeh is more like a dense pancake than a frittata. Called havitat yerek in Hebrew (literally, "omelet with greens"), it is sold, stuffed into pitas, at many roadside eateries and falafel joints. But the real thing, which also contains ground meat, is found almost exclusively in Syrian (Aleppan) homes. Delicious and so easy to make, this is one of my favorite lunch fixes. It is also great for sandwiches and picnics. Finally, ijeh is a wonderful alternative to the traditional Hanukkah latkes with a big plus: unlike potato latkes, ijeh can be made in advance and served at room temperature.

Makes 15 to 20 pancakes

For the pancakes

4 eggs

1 large onion, roughly chopped

About 2 tablespoons matzo meal or bread crumbs

1 bunch fresh parsley

1 bunch fresh cilantro

½ bunch fresh mint

3 to 4 scallions (white and green parts)

10 ounces (300 g) ground beef, or a lamb and beef mixture

Salt and freshly ground black pepper

2 to 3 tablespoons pine nuts (optional)

Vegetable oil for frying

To serve (optional)

Pita, bread rolls, or ciabatta

Olive oil

Slices of red onion

Chopped fresh herbs, such as parsley or cilantro

Tomato slices

Tahini spread (see page 159)

1. **Prepare the pancakes** Put the eggs, onion, matzo meal or bread crumbs, parsley, cilantro, mint, and scallions in a food processor. Pulse until the herbs are chopped. Transfer to a bowl.

2. Add the ground beef, salt, pepper, and pine nuts (if using) and mix thoroughly.

3. Heat a little bit of vegetable oil in a large nonstick frying pan. With a large spoon, ladle in pancakes 3 inches (7 cm) wide and fry over medium heat for 3 to 4 minutes on each side, until deep golden. Be careful not to crowd the pan (work in batches). Remove to paper towels to drain.

4. **To serve** If desired, brush the pita with olive oil and toast in a hot pan or oven. Arrange the pancakes on the bread (it will absorb the flavorful juices) and top with red onion, herbs, tomato, and tahini spread. If not serving at once, store the pancakes in the refrigerator—they are delicious cold or at room temperature in a sandwich or as a light snack.

VARIATION

FOR A VEGETARIAN VERSION Skip the meat. Increase the amount of matzo meal or bread crumbs to 5 tablespoons. You might also want to add 1 to 2 chopped and slowly sautéed onions for extra flavor.

GEFILTE FISH

I once read about an Ashkenazi rabbi who claimed that the smell of the gefilte fish cooking in his wife's kitchen was to him like the smell of paradise. What can I say? He must have loved his wife and her cooking very much. Though crazy about gefilte, I make sure all the windows are wide open while it is cooking.

"Gefilte" means "stuffed" in Yiddish, and indeed the classic recipe calls for fish slices with their cavities filled with minced fish patties. Today the vast majority of cooks make do with just fish patties.

The following recipe was given to me by Shmil Holland, a wonderful chef and a true champion of Ashkenazi cuisine. His version contains ground almonds that enrich the texture (especially beneficial when using leaner fish), and he cooks the stock separately. The very first time I made it, it turned out just the way I like it—light, subtly seasoned, not too fishy, yet authentic. In Eastern Europe, pike or oily, flavorful carp is used for gefilte, but you may also use other white-fleshed varieties, such as whitefish. To streamline the preparation, ask the fishmonger to fillet and mince the fish and to reserve the bones, skins, and heads for the stock in a separate container.

Serves 8 to 10

For the stock

Bones, skins, and heads from the fish used to make the patties (see below)

5 carrots

3 onions

1 leek (white and light green parts)

1 parsley root, peeled (if you can't find it, substitute a parsnip)

1 celery root (celeriac), peeled and quartered

8 fresh thyme sprigs (optional)

4 tablespoons sugar

1 teaspoon black peppercorns

6 allspice berries

3 bay leaves

1 tablespoon coarse salt

4 quarts (4 L) water

1 bunch fresh parsley

1 bunch fresh dill

1. **To prepare the stock** Place the reserved fish parts, carrots, onions, leek, parsley root, celery root, thyme (if using), sugar, peppercorns, allspice, bay leaves, and salt in a large pot. Add the water and bring to a boil. Cover and simmer gently for 50 minutes, skimming occasionally. Add the parsley and dill and cook for 10 minutes more.

2. Remove from the heat, allow to cool, and strain through a fine sieve. Reserve the carrots and 1 onion, and discard the rest of the vegetables.

3. **To prepare the patties** Puree the reserved cooked onion and 4 cooked carrots (reserve 1 for garnish) in a food processor. Transfer to a large bowl, add the minced fish, and mix thoroughly.

4. Add the matzo meal, almonds, eggs, sugar, allspice, salt, and pepper and mix thoroughly. Add ½ cup stock (make sure it's cold; otherwise the eggs will curdle) and knead thoroughly. Cover the bowl with plastic wrap and transfer to the refrigerator for at least 1 hour.

5. Bring the strained stock to a boil in a large wide pot. Make one very small patty and test cook in the broth for a few minutes. Cool slightly, taste, and adjust seasoning, if necessary. The gefilte fish is served cold, and low temperatures tend to mute the flavors. Make sure, therefore, that the sweet-salty-peppery flavors are pronounced and nicely balanced.

6. With wet hands, form elliptical patties 2 to 3 inches long and slide them into the boiling stock. Simmer over medium heat for 30 minutes in a partly covered pot. The patties should fit in the pot in a single layer—if there is not enough room, cook them in two batches. Remove the cooked patties with a

For the fish patties

2 pounds (1 kg) skinless fillet of carp, pike, or whitefish, minced

3 tablespoons matzo meal

4 tablespoons finely ground almonds

2 eggs

2 to 3 tablespoons sugar

2 teaspoons freshly ground allspice

1½ tablespoons salt

1 teaspoon freshly ground black pepper or to taste

slotted spoon and transfer to a wide dish. Strain the stock twice and pour over the patties until they are submerged. Reserve the rest of the stock in a separate container. Refrigerate both overnight. The stock will congeal into the famous gefilte jelly.

7. Garnish each patty with a slice of cooked carrot and arrange on a platter. Serve with some jellied stock and chrain (horseradish dipping sauce; see below).

TO MAKE CHRAIN Combine 7 ounces (200 g) peeled and finely grated horseradish root with 1 small peeled and finely grated beetroot. Season with 6 tablespoons white or red wine vinegar (balsamic vinegar can be used as well), 3 tablespoons sugar or honey, and 1 teaspoon salt. Chrain will keep, refrigerated, for about 1 week.

CRISPY FISH CAKES WITH PINE NUTS AND FRESH HERBS

TURKISH

These spicy, crunchy snacks are delicious with lemon wedges or thick yogurt. Normally you would mince the fish (ask the fishmonger to do it, or briefly pulse fish fillets in the food processor), however, chopping the flesh with a knife adds texture and makes every bite more succulent.

Makes 25 to 30 patties

For the fish cakes

1¾ pounds (750 g) meaty white fish, such as cod, tilapia, or halibut, pulsed until coarsely chopped in a food processor or coarsely chopped with a sharp knife

2 tablespoons pine nuts, ground in a mortar and pestle or a mini food processor, plus 2 tablespoons whole

2 fresh dill sprigs, finely chopped

5 fresh parsley sprigs, finely chopped

2 garlic cloves, crushed

1 large onion, finely chopped

2 eggs

2 tablespoons good quality bread crumbs (or slightly more, as needed)

Zest of 1 lemon

¼ cup fresh lemon juice

Dash of Tabasco sauce or ½ hot chile pepper (red or green), finely chopped

Salt and freshly ground black pepper

For coating and frying

1 cup best-quality bread crumbs (I like Japanese panko crumbs best)

Vegetable oil for frying

1. Prepare the fish cakes Combine the fish, ground pine nuts, whole pine nuts, dill, parsley, garlic, onion, eggs, bread crumbs, lemon zest, lemon juice, Tabasco, salt, and pepper and knead thoroughly. Refrigerate for 1 to 2 hours to stabilize.

2. With wet hands, form balls 1½ inches (4 cm) in diameter and flatten them slightly. Coat with the 1 cup bread crumbs.

3. Heat about 1 inch (2½ cm) of vegetable oil in a frying pan. Fry the patties in batches, 2 to 3 minutes on each side, until golden. Transfer to a paper towel–lined plate.

4. Serve hot or at room temperature. The patties can be made a few hours in advance and heated, covered with aluminum foil, in a 350°F (180°C) oven for 5 to 6 minutes.

HOMEMADE PICKLED HERRING

Sure, you can buy pickled herring in Jewish delicatessens, but making it at home is so easy! Prepare a large batch, store in nice glass jars, and take to your foodie friends— they will appreciate the gesture!

Makes 2 pounds (1 kg) herring

2½ cups water

1⅔ cups distilled vinegar or white wine vinegar

1 tablespoon sugar

2 pounds (1 kg) herring fillets or matjes/matias (available at Jewish and Eastern European delis), cut into 4 pieces each

2 pounds (1 kg) red onions, thinly sliced

2 to 3 scallions (white and green parts), sliced

10 bay leaves

5 allspice berries

10 black peppercorns

1. Mix the water, vinegar, and sugar in a bowl until the sugar dissolves.

2. In a clean, sterilized glass jar, arrange layers of fish fillets, red onions, scallions, bay leaves, allspice, and peppercorns. Pour in the vinegar mixture to cover. Seal the jars and refrigerate for 48 hours. Drizzle some oil before serving. The pickled herring will keep for 2 months in the fridge.

TO MAKE PICKLED HERRING SALAD Dice 2 or 3 of the pickled herring fillets, mix with 2 tablespoons chopped fresh dill, 3 tablespoons chopped red onion, 3 tablespoons chopped scallions, ¾ cup sour cream or thick yogurt, and 2 tablespoons mayonnaise. Season with freshly ground black pepper (no salt is needed; the fillets are salty enough) and mix well.

SELIODKA POD SHUBOY | Layered Beet and Herring Salad

RUSSIAN

The name of this dish, literally meaning "herring under a fur coat," refers to the way it is constructed: Herring pieces are hidden under a thick and colorful coat of beets, potatoes, onions, and eggs, with mayonnaise squirted between the layers. You can forgo the layers and just mix everything together, but then it won't be a fur coat, just a salad. In my childhood home in Riga, this was the star of the zakuski table.

Serves 8 to 10

4 red potatoes

2 to 3 medium beets

4 herring fillets or matjes/matias (available at Jewish and Eastern European delis), cut into ½-inch (1-cm) pieces

2 onions, thinly sliced (optional)

¾ to 1 cup mayonnaise (preferably homemade)

3 hard-boiled eggs, plus 1 for garnish

1. Bring 2 large pots of salted water to a boil. Cook the potatoes and beets separately until tender but still firm. Cool and peel (use gloves when peeling beets, to prevent your hands and nails from turning purple).

2. Select a large, flat serving platter and arrange the fish pieces evenly on it. If using onions, sprinkle them over the fish. Using a squeeze bottle, squirt a thin layer of mayonnaise over the fish and onions and smooth with a spatula.

3. Grate the boiled potatoes on a coarse grater over the herring and use a fork to spread evenly. Cover with another thin layer of mayonnaise.

4. Continue in the same manner with layers of the eggs and the beets, spreading a thin coat of mayonnaise between them.

5. To decorate: Divide the remaining egg into white and yolk and grate separately for garnish. Sprinkle half of the surface with egg yolk and the other half with egg white. Refrigerate for 2 to 4 hours before serving.

VARIATIONS

• Replace some of the mayonnaise with sour cream (in equal proportions or to taste).

• Add a layer of tart apples, peeled and coarsely chopped or finely diced.

• Instead of creating layers, mix the ingredients to make a salad. In this case, it is preferable to dice the beets, onions, eggs, and potatoes. The salad will have a bright pink color.

FORSCHMAK | Herring-Apple Pâté

ASHKENAZI

Herring, tart apples, onions, and sour cream is a classic Eastern European combination that is usually served as a kind of deli salad. Here they are blended into a mousselike spread. In German and Yiddish, forschmak (sometimes spelled *vorschmack*) simply means "appetizer," which is exactly what it is, served with challah or on toast.

Serves 6 to 8

4 herring fillets or matjes/matias (available at Jewish and Eastern European delis)

1 tart apple, peeled, seeded, and chopped

¾ cup sour cream

2 hard-boiled eggs

2 slices white bread or challah, crust removed

1 onion, coarsely chopped

1 tablespoon white wine vinegar

Salt

Place the herring, apple, sour cream, hard-boiled eggs, bread, onion, and vinegar in a food processor and process until completely smooth and the texture is like that of a mousse. Add a little salt, if necessary. Serve or keep refrigerated for a day or two.

VARIATIONS

• Add 1 tablespoon sugar to deepen the flavors.

• **YIDDISHE SALSA** Dice the herring, apple, and onion into tiny cubes. Process the remaining ingredients and mix with the herring, apple, and onion to achieve a chunkier texture reminiscent of salsa.

MESSAYIR | Pickled Salad

Crunchy, colorful, and zesty, this salad keeps well in the fridge. To streamline the preparation, julienne the vegetables in a food processor or with a mandoline (use a julienne blade).

Serves 10 to 12

2 carrots, cut into matchsticks (juliennes)

2 kohlrabis, cut into matchsticks (juliennes)

3 celery stalks, without leaves, cut into matchsticks (juliennes)

2 fennel bulbs, thinly sliced

¼ head cauliflower, separated into small florets

½ fresh hot chile pepper (red or green), seeded and thinly sliced

1 lemon, halved and thinly sliced

1 teaspoon salt, or more to taste

¼ cup fresh lemon juice

Toss the carrots, kohlrabis, celery, fennel, cauliflower, chile, lemon, salt, and lemon juice thoroughly in a bowl. Taste and adjust the seasoning. Let stand for at least 30 minutes before serving. After 3 or 4 hours, it will be even tastier. The salad can be kept in the fridge for 3 to 4 days.

CHERSHI | Lemony Pumpkin Spread

LIBYAN (TRIPOLITAN)

Brilliantly orange, tangy, spicy, garlicky, and—as with many dishes from this cuisine—laced with oil, chershi is traditionally served as a garnish for couscous, but is delicious on its own. Feel free to reduce the amount of oil—in fact, low-fat chershi makes a delicious diet-friendly sandwich spread.

Serves 8 to 10

4 pounds (1½ kg) pumpkin or butternut squash, peeled and cut into 2-inch (5-cm) cubes

⅔ cup fresh lemon juice

8 garlic cloves, minced

1 teaspoon ground cumin

1 tablespoon (or more to taste) harissa (page 7 or store-bought)

Salt

½ to ¾ cup extra virgin olive oil

I. Put the pumpkin in a large pot and add water to cover. Bring to a boil and cook for about 30 minutes, until it is completely soft. Transfer to a colander and let stand only until the pumpkin is cool enough to handle with bare hands.

2. Thoroughly squeeze out the liquid (the drier it is, the better the dish will taste). If the pumpkin has cooled completely, warm for a couple minutes in a microwave (warm vegetables absorb seasoning more effectively).

3. Add the lemon juice, garlic, cumin, harissa, and salt. Mix well and adjust the seasoning—the spread should be fairly spicy and really tart. Add the olive oil and mix well. Serve at room temperature. Chershi will keep in the fridge for 3 to 4 days.

VARIATIONS

• Instead of boiling the pumpkin, roast it on a parchment–lined baking sheet at 400°F (200°C) for 20 to 30 minutes, until very soft. In this case, there will be no need to squeeze out the liquid.

• Replace half of the pumpkin with a combination of cooked carrots and sweet potatoes, peeled and cut into large chunks.

APIO | Celeriac and Carrots in Lemon Sauce

TURKISH, BALKAN

Delicate and lemony, tender with a bit of a bite, this classic Sephardic cooked salad is lovely as a starter or a side. It is usually reserved for festive occasions, mainly Passover, when celery root is at its peak.

Serves 4 to 6

4 large celery roots (celeriacs), peeled, quartered, and sliced into ⅓-inch (1-cm)-thick pieces

2 carrots, sliced into ⅓-inch (1-cm)-thick pieces

2 tablespoons olive oil

1 cup water

Juice of 2 lemons

Salt and freshly ground black pepper

Dash of sugar

Chopped celery leaves

1. Put the celery root and carrots in a medium saucepan with the olive oil and heat over low heat for 2 to 3 minutes.

2. Add the water, lemon juice, salt, pepper, and sugar. Cook for 45 minutes over low heat, or until the vegetables are tender but still retain some bite.

3. Remove the vegetables with a slotted spoon, reduce the sauce until very thick, almost like aloe vera gel. Return the vegetables to the pan, taste, and adjust the seasoning; the vegetables should be tart.

4. Transfer to a serving dish and allow to cool. Garnish with chopped celery leaves before serving.

VARIATIONS

• Add 1 cup quartered or halved artichoke hearts along with the celery root and carrots.

• Use unsalted butter instead of olive oil.

• Use chicken stock instead of water.

• Instead of sugar, add a little honey, date honey (silan; see page 147), or maple syrup.

Cozy Soups for Chilly Nights

One of my earliest food memories is sitting at my grandmother's kitchen table, dutifully slurping chicken soup with tons of noodles, while she watches over me like a hawk and urges me to have bread with the soup (a habit I cannot shake to this very day). As a child I found eating soup tedious—spoonful after spoonful; it seemed like the bowl was bottomless. Today soup is my ultimate comfort food. I love cooking it, I love eating it, and most of all, I revel in knowing that there is a pot of homemade soup waiting for me and my family as we gather for dinner on a winter's night.

KRUPNIK | Mushroom and Barley Soup

ASHKENAZI

This peasant soup is common in Russian and Polish cuisines, where it usually contains meat. In kosher households, it is usually prepared without meat (pareve), to make it suitable for all kinds of meals. Better yet, since it is pareve, you can serve it with a spoonful of sour cream, which makes it so much better. The dry porcini mushrooms compensate for wild forest mushrooms—the secret culinary treasure of Eastern European cuisines.

Serves 6 to 8

Small handful (½ ounce/15 g) dried porcini mushrooms

1 tablespoon vegetable oil

2 onions, finely chopped

2 small or 1 large parsley roots or parsnips, peeled and finely chopped

1 celery root (celeriac), peeled and finely chopped

2 carrots, finely chopped

3 garlic cloves, finely chopped

1 pound (½ kilogram) white button mushrooms (caps only), thinly sliced

Salt and freshly ground black pepper

6 to 7 cups water

Bouquet garni: parsley, dill, and thyme, tied with a kitchen string

2 potatoes, peeled and diced

½ cup pearl barley, rinsed

Pinch of freshly grated nutmeg (optional)

1 cup sour cream or thick yogurt

1. Soak the porcini mushrooms in 1 cup hot water for 40 minutes (or if you have time, soak for 2 hours in lukewarm water).

2. Heat the vegetable oil in a soup pot over medium heat. Add the onions and sauté for 5 minutes, until translucent. Add the parsley roots, celery root, and carrots and sauté for 2 to 3 minutes. Add the garlic and sauté for 2 to 3 minutes.

3. Remove the porcini from the soaking liquid. Squeeze out the liquid from the mushrooms into the soaking liquid. Strain the soaking liquid through a fine sieve and reserve. Coarsely chop the rehydrated porcini. Add the button mushrooms and porcini mushrooms to the pot and sauté for 2 to 3 minutes. Season with salt and pepper.

4. Add the water. Carefully pour in the reserved mushroom soaking liquid, making sure no sediment makes it into the pot. Add the bouquet garni. Bring to a boil and cook for 5 minutes. Add the potatoes and barley and return to a boil. Cover, reduce the heat, and simmer for 30 minutes, skimming the foam occasionally.

5. Season with nutmeg (if using), and more salt and pepper, if necessary. Leave covered for 15 minutes. Serve with a dollop of sour cream.

VARIATIONS

- Sprinkle with chopped fresh dill before serving.

- Replace some of the potatoes with cauliflower florets.

- Add 1 diced zucchini along with the barley and potatoes.

ISRAELI CHICKEN SOUP

Chicken soup is an emotional matter. Passed down from one's bubbe, this is not a recipe to mess with. Both my grandmothers made superb goldene yoich, but they had passed away long before I got into cooking. The following recipe is the sum total of tips, ideas, warnings, and variations I learned over the years from Israeli cooks of diverse roots—Polish, Russian, Romanian, Balkan, and even Moroccan. It is not classically Ashkenazi, but it is delicious, uplifting, and comforting. During colder months, I make it almost every week. Pay attention to the "herbs trick": Half of them are placed at the bottom of the pot, to prevent them from floating into the soup and clouding it; the rest are added at the very end for a boost of fresh fragrance.

Serves 8 to 10

1 large bunch fresh dill

1 large bunch fresh parsley

5 to 6 celery stalks, with leaves

2 pounds (1 kg) chicken parts or 1 small whole chicken

1 turkey neck, cut into a few chunks

1 large onion

3 carrots, halved lengthwise

1 leek, cut into large chunks

1 celery root (celeriac), quartered

1 parsley root or parsnip, halved lengthwise

2 zucchini or summer squash, cut into large chunks

½ pound (250 g) pumpkin or butternut squash, cut into large chunks

1 whole tomato

3 quarts (3 L) water

1 teaspoon black peppercorns

3 to 4 allspice berries

2 to 3 bay leaves

Salt

1. Line the bottom of a large soup pot with half of the dill, parsley, and celery. Arrange the chicken, turkey, onion, carrots, leek, celery root, parsley root, zucchini, pumpkin, and tomato over the herbs and pour in the water. Add the peppercorns, allspice, and bay leaves.

2. Bring to a boil, skim the foam, and reduce the heat. Simmer, partially covered, for 1½ to 2 hours.

3. Season with salt only toward the end of the cooking (especially if you are using kosher chicken, which tends to be salty). Tie the rest of the herbs in a bundle and add to the pot for the last 5 minutes of cooking.

4. If you plan to use the chicken for other recipes (salads, sandwiches), remove it from the soup after 1½ hours to retain its texture and succulence.

5. Cool the soup for 30 minutes and strain. Discard the herbs and keep the carrots, celery root, parsley root, leek, onion, zucchini, pumpkin, and tomato in a separate container. You might want to serve them with the soup.

SERVING SUGGESTIONS

Add one or more of the following:

• Cooked chicken meat (from the soup) removed from the bones and shredded by hand into little pieces

• Freshly chopped dill

• Chunks of cooked vegetables (from the soup)

• Vermicelli or other small noodles (boiled separately according to the instructions on the package and added to the hot soup at the last moment)

KNEIDLACH | Matzo Balls

ASHKENAZI

Matzo balls are tricky. The preparation doesn't appear to be complicated at all, but too often, rather than being fluffy and flavorful, matzo balls turn out dense and bland tasting. Hadassah Kavel (see page 43) inherited this recipe from her mother, Leah. The secret ingredient in Leah's kneidlach was onions fried to sweetness. Hadassah improved on it by adding fresh herbs.

Makes 20 to 25 dumplings

¼ cup vegetable oil

1 medium onion, finely chopped

1 cup matzo meal

1½ cups boiling water mixed with 3 tablespoons vegetable oil

2 eggs, beaten

Salt and freshly ground black pepper

Dash of ground nutmeg

Leaves from 6 to 7 fresh parsley sprigs, finely chopped

Leaves from 6 to 7 fresh dill sprigs, finely chopped

Leaves from 6 to 7 fresh cilantro sprigs, finely chopped

I. Heat the vegetable oil in a skillet over medium-low heat. Add the onion and sauté until golden, 8 to 9 minutes. Set aside, with the oil.

2. Put the matzo meal in a bowl and pour the boiling water mixture over it. Whisk vigorously and cool slightly. Stir in the eggs, salt, pepper, nutmeg, onion and oil, parsley, dill, and cilantro. Cool to room temperature.

3. Fill a large pot with water, add 1 teaspoon salt for every quart of water, and bring to a boil.

4. With wet hands, form dumplings the size of a walnut (Hadassah prefers them torpedo shaped). Slide them into the boiling water (in two or three batches; don't crowd the pot) and cook for 10 minutes. Serve in a piping-hot chicken soup (3 or 4 balls per serving). You can also boil the kneidlach in the soup. This will add flavor, but the soup will turn a bit cloudy.

MAKING AHEAD

Kneidlach are at their best if cooked on the same day (ideally up to 4 hours before they are served). But, if necessary, it is possible to keep cooked dumplings in an airtight container in the fridge for up to 3 days. Warm them with the soup or separately.

PASSOVER GREEN CHICKEN SOUP

ALGERIAN

Hadassah Kavel was born in Romania and grew up in Israel, but in her extended family she is considered the ultimate authority on Jewish Algerian cooking. She earned this reputation during forty years of marriage to Gerard, an Algerian Jew, who is as much into cooking as she is. Their famous Seder meals celebrate the best of Jewish Algerian cuisine with some add-ons from Hadassah's own culinary legacy.

Soups with fava beans and green vegetables are a must at the Seder table of North African Jews. Usually diners break matzo into the soup to make it more substantial, but Hadassah prefers to serve the soup with her famous matzo balls (see page 41).

Serves 10 to 12

1 whole chicken (3 pounds/1½ kg), separated into 8 pieces

1 turkey neck, cut into a few chunks

3 cardamom pods

3 bay leaves

10 allspice berries

2 large fresh sage leaves

5 small onions

4 to 5 carrots, sliced into 1-inch (2½-cm) coins

1 celery root (celeriac), quartered

1 fennel bulb (only the outer leaves)

1 cabbage stalk (the hard part without the leaves)

1 small bunch fresh dill

1 small bunch fresh cilantro

1 small bunch fresh parsley

3 to 4 celery stalks, with leaves

¾ cup peeled fava beans, fresh or frozen

½ cup garden peas, fresh or frozen

1. Fill a large pot (about 8 quarts/8 L) three-quarters full with boiling water. Add the chicken pieces and turkey neck and boil for 5 minutes. Drain, save the meat, and wash the pot.

2. Return the meat to the pot and add fresh cold water so that it reaches three-quarters of its volume. Put the cardamom, bay leaves, and allspice in a piece of cloth and tie in a bundle. Add to the pot. Add the sage, onions, carrots, celery root, fennel, and cabbage and bring to a boil. Reduce the heat and simmer for 1 hour. Remove from the heat and cool slightly.

3. Drain the liquid through a fine sieve and pour the broth back into the pot. Save the chicken and cooked vegetables in separate containers. Up to this point, the soup can be made ahead and refrigerated for up to 3 days.

4. When ready to serve, bring the broth to a boil. Tie the dill, cilantro, parsley, and celery in a bundle and add to the broth. Add the fava beans and peas. Return to a boil and simmer for 15 minutes. Remove and discard the herbs. Serve with pieces of matzo or with matzo balls.

THE DAY AFTER SEDER SALAD Hadassah doesn't serve chicken and vegetables with the soup but saves them for the lunch she serves on the first day of the Passover week: Separate the chicken meat from the bones while it is still warm (it is easier that way) and shred it into small pieces. Chop the cooked carrot (from the soup). Add freshly chopped onions and capers and dress with mayonnaise (preferably homemade) seasoned with mustard and minced garlic.

GONDI NOHODI | Chickpea and Chicken Dumplings in Turmeric-Lime Broth

PERSIAN

We first met at Eden, a modest Persian restaurant in downtown Tel Aviv. A couple of biggish, grayish dumplings, looking like matzo balls on steroids, sat in the middle of a vividly yellow broth. I took one tentative bite and fell in love. Meaty, exotically spiced, their texture succulent yet light, gondi dumplings were a revelation.

As with most ethnic recipes, there are immense variations in cooking techniques. This recipe is quite straightforward and yields fluffy and flavorful dumplings. To make it, you will need toasted chickpea flour, available at health food stores, Indian groceries, and spice shops. Another unique ingredient is lemon omani—Persian dried lime. Almost black and hard, the limes look like lemons that were forgotten for months in the kitchen cabinet. They add elusive smoky tartness to the broth and are worth seeking out, though not a must. They are pretty common in Middle Eastern groceries or you can buy them online (see Mail Order Sources, page 203, for both ingredients).

Serves 6 to 8

For the broth

4 chicken legs (thighs and drumsticks)

1 cup chickpeas, soaked in water overnight

2 onions

2 zucchini or summer squash, cut into large chunks

2 to 3 Persian dried limes (lemon omani; optional)

1 teaspoon ground turmeric

10 cups water

Salt

For the dumplings

1 pound (½ kg) finely ground chicken breast

1 cup toasted chickpea flour (available at spice shops, Indian groceries, and health food stores; see Mail Order Sources, page 203)

3 onions, grated

1 teaspoon ground cardamom

1 teaspoon ground cumin

1 teaspoon ground turmeric

Salt and white pepper

¼ cup vegetable oil

1. Prepare the broth Place the chicken legs, chickpeas, onions, and zucchini in a large pot. Prick the dried limes in a few places with the tip of a knife to release the flavor, then add to the pot. Season with the turmeric. Add the water and bring to a boil. Skim the foam off the top of the broth and cook over low heat for about 1 hour. Taste and season with salt.

2. Meanwhile, prepare the dumplings Mix the ground chicken, chickpea flour, onions, cardamom, cumin, turmeric, salt, white pepper, and vegetable oil and knead thoroughly for 2 to 3 minutes. If the mixture is too dry, add a little bit of water (up to ⅓ cup).

3. Wet your hands or rub them with a bit of oil and form dumplings the size of golf balls (the dumplings will swell considerably during cooking).

4. Remove the chicken legs from the broth and set aside. Slide the dumplings into the simmering broth and return to a boil. Lower the heat and simmer for about 1½ hours with the pot half covered.

5. To serve, pour the broth into serving bowls (not too much, about a third of a bowl). Add some of the reserved chicken legs and 2 or 3 dumplings per serving.

VARIATIONS

• Instead of chickpea flour, use toasted salty chickpeas (available at Indian groceries and health food stores) and grind them in a food processor. This will yield dumplings with a slightly chunky texture. Reduce the salt in the recipe.

• If you skip the dried limes, you may want to serve the soup with lemon wedges.

• It is possible to serve gondi over rice, as a main course. In this case, the broth serves as a sauce rather than a soup.

GONDALACH

ISRAELI

s is gondi? Is it kneidlach? It's gondalach! The ever-creative chef Erez Komarovsky brings together dispersed diasporas in these scrumptious and easy-to-make dumplings. You can replace the slightly bitter arugula with the same amount of chopped scallions. Erez cooks and serves the gondalach in a traditional chicken soup with some personal trimmings (such as shredded spinach, which he adds just before serving), but any homemade chicken soup is fit for the task.

Makes about 40 small dumplings; serves 10 to 12

1 pound (½ kg) ground chicken breast

¾ cup toasted chickpea flour (available at spice shops, Indian groceries, and health food stores, and online; see Mail Order Sources, page 203)

1 to 2 eggs

¼ teaspoon baking soda

1 cup arugula leaves, finely chopped

½ cup scallions (white and green parts), finely chopped

¼ teaspoon ground turmeric

¼ teaspoon ground cardamom

¼ teaspoon ground caraway

½ teaspoon white pepper

Salt

About 3½ quarts (3 L) flavorful chicken soup, for cooking the gondalach (see, for example, page 40)

1. Put the chicken, chickpea flour, 1 egg, baking soda, arugula, scallions, turmeric, cardamom, caraway, white pepper, and salt in a large bowl and knead for 2 to 3 minutes until soft and thoroughly combined. If the mixture is too thick, add another egg. Let rest in the refrigerator for 30 minutes.

2. Bring the chicken soup to a boil.

3. With wet hands, form dumplings the size of a walnut and slide them into the soup. Cover and simmer for 30 to 40 minutes.

4. To serve, pour the soup into soup bowls, with 3 to 4 gondalach per serving.

LENTIL STEW WITH CUMIN, GARLIC, AND CORIANDER

SYRIAN (ALEPPAN)

first tasted this soup at Bertie, one of my favorite restaurants in Tel Aviv. It was cold and rainy outside, and a bowl of hot, thick, fragrant soup was a perfect fit. So much so, that I approached Roi Antebi, chef and one of the owners, and asked for the recipe. It was so simple, I didn't even need to write it down. The brilliant combination of cumin, garlic, and coriander seeds, along with freshly squeezed lemon juice, makes the flavor.

Serves 8 to 10

3 tablespoons olive oil

3 onions, thinly chopped

2 tablespoons coriander seeds

1 teaspoon cumin seeds

10 garlic cloves, thinly sliced

2 pounds (1 kg) yellow or orange lentils

3 quarts (3 L) water or chicken stock

½ cup fresh lemon juice

1 large bunch fresh cilantro (tied)

Salt and freshly ground black pepper

Chopped fresh cilantro (optional)

Croutons (optional)

1. Heat the olive oil in a large soup pot over medium heat. Add the onions and sauté for 5 to 6 minutes, until translucent.

2. Crush the coriander and cumin seeds in a mortar and pestle and add to the pot. Add the garlic and sauté for 3 to 4 minutes, until very fragrant.

3. Add the lentils and water. Bring to a boil, lower the heat, and simmer until the lentils are soft and almost dissolved into the liquid.

4. Add the lemon juice. Tie the cilantro in a bundle and add to the pot. Taste and season with salt and pepper. Cook for 10 more minutes. Remove the tied cilantro. To serve, pour into bowls and garnish with chopped cilantro and croutons, if desired.

TIP

Legume soups (lentil, bean, chickpea) thicken considerably in the fridge. Add more water or stock when reheating.

The Magic of Lemon

Most soups taste better a day or two after they are cooked. And the reason: They sour slightly in the refrigerator, and this cuts through the earthiness of the starchy vegetables, legumes, and grains that form the base of most winter soups. Middle Eastern cooks don't wait for the soup to go sour—they squeeze fresh lemon juice during or after cooking, which adds tartness, while also adding a citrusy scent. In Eastern European cuisines, a spoonful of sour cream does the job (see Krupnik, page 39).

BORSCHT | Beet, Cabbage, and Beef Soup

RUSSIAN, UKRAINIAN

In Israel (and North America, for that matter), borscht refers to a beet soup, served hot or chilled. In Russia and the Ukraine, its homeland, borscht is a much more elaborate affair, containing, in addition to beets, a variety of vegetables (notably cabbage), as well as chunks of beef and marrow bones. The following version should be consumed with thick slabs of rye bread.

Serves 8 to 10

¼ cup vegetable oil

3 onions, roughly chopped

1 leek (white and light green parts), roughly chopped

2 pounds (1 kg) lean beef chuck, meaty bone-in shank, beef flanken, or short ribs (depending on the amount of fat you prefer), cut into large chunks

2 marrow bones

Salt and freshly ground black pepper

2 tablespoons dark brown sugar

4 to 5 celery stalks, with the leaves, roughly chopped

3 quarts (3 L) water

½ head red cabbage, roughly chopped

2 to 3 beets, peeled and coarsely sliced

1. Heat the vegetable oil in an ovenproof pot over medium-high heat. Add the onions, leek, meat, and bones. Cook for 5 minutes, or until browned. Season with salt, pepper, and brown sugar and stir well. Add the celery and cook, stirring, for 2 to 3 minutes.

2. Add the water, cabbage, and beets. Bring to a boil, skimming the foam occasionally. Reduce the heat, cover, and simmer for 1½ hours. Add more water, as necessary, if the soup gets too thick.

3. Preheat the oven to 285°F (140°C).

4. Cover the pot and transfer to the oven. Cook for another hour.

5. Serve piping hot and make sure every diner has a chunk of meat in his or her soup bowl.

VARIATION

Add 2 to 3 potatoes, cut into wedges, for the last hour of cooking.

BATATA HAMOOD | Tart Potato and Celery Broth with Meatballs

SYRIAN (ALEPPAN)

Hamood in Hebrew means "cute," which is why this soup's name brings smiles to the faces of Israelis. In Arabic, however, it means "sour," and this is how this Aleppan soup got its name. Based on potatoes and celery, perfumed with dry and fresh mint, and zinged with fresh lemon, it is light and refreshing. During the week, hamood is usually served over rice. A more elaborate version, reserved for Shabbat, contains kubbe dumplings (like the ones on page 52). The following version, containing meatballs, falls somewhere in between: Easier than kubbe to make, meatballs add substance and flavor to the soup. Ruth Oliver, who contributed this recipe, told me that hamood with meatballs was a regular Friday lunch offering in the household of her mother, a twentieth-generation Jerusalemite Sephardic.

Serves 6 to 8

For the meatballs

1 onion

1 pound (½ kg) ground beef

2 tablespoons good-quality plain bread crumbs or matzo meal

3 tablespoons rice

⅓ cup fresh cilantro leaves, chopped

Salt and freshly ground black pepper

For the soup

3 tablespoons vegetable oil

2 onions, cut into 1-inch (2½-cm) cubes

1 bunch celery (stalks and leaves chopped separately)

8 garlic cloves, thinly sliced

2 tablespoons (or more) dried mint

2 quarts (2 L) chicken stock or water

5 medium potatoes, peeled and cut into 1-inch (2½-cm) cubes

½ cup fresh mint, chopped

Salt and freshly ground black pepper

⅓ to ½ cup fresh lemon juice

Lemon wedges

1. Prepare the meatballs Grate the onion on a coarse grater and squeeze out the excess liquid.

2. Mix the grated onion with the beef, bread crumbs, rice, cilantro, salt, and pepper. Knead thoroughly and refrigerate for 30 minutes.

3. Prepare the soup Heat the vegetable oil in a large soup pot over medium heat. Add the onions, chopped celery stalks, and garlic and sauté for 5 to 6 minutes. Add the dried mint and sauté for another minute.

4. Pour in the stock and add the potatoes, fresh mint, and celery leaves. Cook for 30 minutes. Toward the end of the cooking, season with salt and pepper and add the lemon juice. Taste and adjust the seasoning.

5. With wet hands, form meatballs the size of walnuts. Bring the soup to a rapid boil and slide in the meatballs. Return to a boil, reduce the heat, and simmer, partially covered, for 30 minutes. Let stand for 10 minutes before serving. Serve with lemon wedges and encourage diners to squeeze more lemon juice to taste.

VARIATION

HAMOOD SOUP WITH RICE Ladle 3 to 4 tablespoons cooked rice into each serving bowl and pour in the soup. In this case, you can skip the meatballs, but the combination of the two, if you can do both, is tasty and filling.

H'RIRA | Spiced Vegetables and Legume Soup

MOROCCAN

H'rira has its roots in Muslim Moroccan cuisine, where it is a popular dish served to break the Ramadan fast, but the Jews of Morocco fell in love with it and adapted it to their kitchens. What sets h'rira apart is the dominant spice blend. Called ras el hanout, literally "head of the shop," in Arabic, it can contain as many as fifteen spices, with every spice-shop owner having his or her own secret recipe. If you'd like to make your own mix, use the recipe below. Otherwise, look for it in Middle Eastern groceries and gourmet stores (or see Mail Order Sources, page 203). This recipe was developed by Orly Pely-Bronstein, a renowned Israeli cookbook author.

Serves 10 to 12

2 beef shank bones

4 to 5 tablespoons vegetable oil

1 pound (½ kg) stewing beef with a little fat, such as chuck or brisket, cut into large chunks

2 large onions, chopped

2 carrots, chopped

2 celery stalks, chopped

3 garlic cloves, chopped

One 28-oz (800-g) can chopped tomatoes

1 cup dried chickpeas, soaked overnight, or 2 cups canned and drained

1 cup green lentils

1 to 1½ tablespoons ras el hanout spice mix (see below or store-bought)

1 tablespoon tomato paste

4 quarts (4 L) water

3½ ounces (100 g) thin noodles (vermicelli) or ½ cup rice

Dash of sugar

⅓ cup unbleached all-purpose flour

1 cup chopped fresh cilantro

1 cup chopped fresh parsley

Lemon wedges

1. Preheat the oven to 400°F (200°C).

2. Put the shank bones on a baking sheet lined with parchment and roast until browned, about 20 minutes.

3. Heat the oil in a large soup pot over medium heat. Add the stewing meat and brown on all sides. Transfer to a plate. Add the onions, carrots, and celery to the pot and sauté for 2 minutes, scraping the brown bits on the bottom with a wooden spoon. Add the garlic and sauté for 2 minutes. Add the tomatoes, roasted shank bones, browned meat, chickpeas, and lentils and stir well.

4. Add 1 tablespoon of the spice mix, the tomato paste, and water and bring to a boil. Reduce the heat to the minimum and cook, covered, for 2½ hours.

5. Add the noodles and cook for 10 minutes (if using rice, cook for 20 minutes). Taste, add a little sugar to balance the acidity, and, if needed, more of the spice mix. To thicken the soup, mix the flour with 1 cup hot soup. Stir well, pour the mixture back into the soup, and stir to combine.

6. Ladle into soup bowls, sprinkle with the cilantro and parsley, and serve with lemon wedges on the side.

Ras el Hanout Spice Mix

If you make this spice mix, prepare a large batch. Keep it in an airtight container in a cool, dark place. Use it to flavor soups and stews.

¼ cup sweet paprika	½ teaspoon ground allspice
1 teaspoon chili powder	½ teaspoon ground nutmeg
1 teaspoon ground coriander	½ teaspoon ground mace
1 teaspoon ground cumin	½ teaspoon ground ginger
1 teaspoon salt	½ teaspoon ground cinnamon
1 teaspoon freshly ground black pepper	½ teaspoon ground turmeric
½ teaspoon white pepper	½ teaspoon saffron threads

Mix all the ingredients in a bowl. Store in an airtight container in a cool, dark place.

MEAT KUBBE WITH A CHEAT

KURDISH, IRAQI

Kubbe (or kibbe) are meat-stuffed semolina and/or bulgur dumplings. Sometimes they are deep-fried, but in Kurdish and Iraqi cuisines they are usually cooked in soups or sauces. There are many variations of the dough with every possible combination of bulgur and semolina and many nuances to the filling. The trickiest part is shaping the dumpling, an art in which Kurdish and Iraqi grandmothers take a special pride.

Grandmas may consider it cheating, but here is a brilliant and user-friendly method in which you assemble the dumplings inside out: Rather than making dough balls, flattening them, stuffing them with the meat mixture, and smoothing them over, you make small meatballs, freeze them, and then wrap them with the dough. Whichever way you make the kubbe, prepare a double batch so you can freeze them and always have delicious dumplings on hand. You can add them to various soups (see the recipes on pages 50, 55, and 57).

To make kubbe dough, you will need semolina and finely milled bulgur. The latter is not found in every supermarket, but is pretty common in gourmet stores, Middle Eastern groceries, and health food stores (see also Mail Order Sources, page 203).

Makes about 30 dumplings

For the dough

2 cups finely milled bulgur

1½ cups water

2 cups plus 2 tablespoons semolina (cream of wheat or cream of farina)

Salt

I. Start the dough Put the bulgur in a bowl and rinse it several times, until the draining water runs clear. Drain in a fine-mesh sieve or strainer and return to the bowl. Add the water, stir, and leave for 30 minutes, or until the water is fully absorbed.

2. Meanwhile, prepare the filling Heat the vegetable oil in a large saucepan over medium heat. Add the onions and sauté until golden, 7 to 8 minutes. Add the meat and season with baharat, salt, and pepper. Stir-fry, crumbling the meat with a fork, until the meat changes color. Taste and adjust the seasoning. Remove from the heat, add the parsley, and allow to cool.

For the filling

¼ cup vegetable oil

2 onions, finely chopped

1 pound (½ kg) ground beef

½ tablespoon baharat spice mix (available at Middle Eastern groceries and spice shops or see page 150)

Salt and freshly ground black pepper

½ cup fresh parsley leaves, finely chopped

3. Make small meatballs 1 inch (2½ cm) in diameter. Arrange on a parchment-lined baking sheet and freeze until solid, about 2 hours.

4. Prepare the dough Mix the semolina and ¾ teaspoon salt into the bowl with the bulgur. Knead with your hands for 7 to 8 minutes, until the dough is smooth and pliable. Add a little semolina or water as needed.

5. Pinch off pieces of dough and shape the dough evenly around the meatballs to create a thin and even shell (that is usually achieved by only the most advanced grandmothers). Use immediately, keep in the refrigerator for a day, or freeze.

VARIATION

TO ASSEMBLE THE KUBBE IN THE TRADITIONAL MANNER Wet your hands and form some of the dough into a golf ball–size ball. Hollow out the center with your thumb and pinch the sides to form a thin bowl. If the dough tears, patch it with a little additional dough. Spoon 2 teaspoons of the filling into the cavity, pinch the dough over to close the opening, seal, and roll it into a smooth ball. Repeat with the rest of the dough and filling.

BEET SOUP WITH KUBBE

IRAQI

There are two genres of this vividly violet soup: one thick and shiny, almost saucelike; the other, thinner and similar in texture to the eastern European beet borscht. I find the latter lighter and more befitting the hearty dumplings. This recipe is from Amir Kronberg, chef-owner of Gedera 26, a charming little restaurant on the outskirts of Hacarmel Market in Tel Aviv. Amir adapted it from his Iraqi grandmother's recipe.

Serves 8 to 10

2 tablespoons vegetable oil

5 medium beets, halved and cut into thin wedges

5 carrots, sliced into 1-inch (2½-cm) coins

1 large onion, chopped

1 large bunch celery (stalks and leaves chopped separately)

2 tablespoons tomato paste

1 tablespoon salt

3 quarts (3 L) water or chicken stock

2 to 3 tablespoons sugar

⅓ to ½ cup fresh lemon juice

20 to 30 kubbe dumplings
(see page 52)

1. Heat the vegetable oil in a large soup pot over medium heat. Sauté the beets, carrots, onion, and celery stalks until the beets start to "bleed," about 10 minutes.

2. Stir in the tomato paste and season with the salt. Add the water and sugar and cook over medium heat for 1 hour.

3. Add the celery leaves and lemon juice. Taste and adjust the seasoning. The soup should have a nicely balanced sour-sweet flavor.

4. Bring the soup to a rapid boil and slide the dumplings into the soup (if you are using frozen ones, there is no need to thaw them). Shake the pot to distribute the dumplings evenly and simmer, partially covered, for 30 minutes. Serve hot.

PUMPKIN SOUP WITH KUBBE

IRAQI

Golden-hued, sweet and sour, and so easy to make! For best results, use good homemade chicken soup, like the one on page 40.

Serves 8 to 10

3½ pounds (1½ kg) pumpkin or butternut squash, peeled and cut into 2-inch (5-cm) cubes

1½ cups canned crushed tomatoes

5 celery stalks, with the leaves, coarsely chopped

Small handful of golden raisins (optional)

1½ quarts (1½ L) chicken stock or homemade chicken soup

2 tablespoons sugar

½ cup fresh lemon juice

Salt and freshly ground black pepper

20 to 30 kubbe dumplings (see page 52)

1. Place the pumpkin, tomatoes, celery, and raisins (if using) in a soup pot. Add the chicken stock and bring to a boil. Reduce the heat and cook, covered, for 20 minutes, or until the pumpkin is tender. Toward the end of cooking, season with the sugar, lemon juice, salt, and pepper.

2. Bring the soup to a rapid boil and slide the dumplings into the soup (if you are using frozen ones, there is no need to thaw them). Shake the pot to distribute the dumplings evenly and simmer, partially covered, for 30 minutes. Serve hot.

Meatballs, Fish Balls, and Stuffed Vegetables

How does one feed a big family with just a little bit of inexpensive meat or chicken? She grinds it, stretches it with bread crumbs, adds spices and herbs, makes meatballs, cooks them in a tasty sauce, and serves them with rice, couscous, or mashed potatoes. Or better yet, she hollows out some seasonal vegetables and stuffs them with ground meat and rice. To paraphrase an old adage, "Frugality is the mother of invention," as these recipes amply show.

ALBONDIGAS | Beef and Grilled Eggplant Meatballs

SEPHARDIC, BALKAN

Al-bunduq means "hazelnut" in Arabic, and in Ladino, albondigas are small meatballs. One of the iconic dishes of Sephardic Jews and the epitome of Jerusalem cuisine, these tiny meatballs are always cooked in rich sauce. In this version, roasted eggplants and bell peppers add subtle smokiness and balance the acidity of the lemon juice and tomato paste.

Serves 6 to 8

For the sauce

3 medium eggplants

2 red bell peppers

5 garlic cloves, crushed

¼ cup fresh lemon juice

1 tablespoon sugar

Salt

2 tablespoons tomato paste

½ cup water

For the meatballs

1 pound (½ kg) ground beef or veal

2 slices white bread, without crusts, soaked in water and squeezed

2 eggs

3 garlic cloves, minced

Salt and freshly ground black pepper

¼ cup chopped fresh herbs, such as parsley or cilantro

3 to 4 tablespoons vegetable oil for frying

1. Prepare the sauce Place the eggplants on a rack over the open flame of the stove. Roast, turning occasionally, until the skins are charred and the flesh feels soft. The eggplants can also be roasted in a hot oven (450°F/250°C) under a broiler or over hot charcoals.

2. Cool slightly to avoid burning your hands. Peel the eggplants, taking care to remove all bits of charred skin, or cut in half lengthwise and scoop out the flesh. Transfer the flesh to a colander to drain, for an hour. Chop the flesh coarsely. Set aside.

3. Place the bell peppers on a rack over the open flame of the stove or under a broiler and roast, turning occasionally, until the skins are charred. Transfer to a plastic container and close. Allow to cool (the skin will separate from the flesh). Peel the skins, remove the seeds and the membranes, and coarsely chop the flesh. Set aside.

4. Prepare the meatballs Combine the meat, bread, eggs, garlic, salt, pepper, and herbs in a large bowl. Knead thoroughly with your hands and refrigerate the mixture for 30 minutes.

5. Preheat the oven to 300°F (150°C).

6. Wet your hands or rub them with oil and form meatballs the size of a walnut.

7. Heat the vegetable oil in a large skillet. Add the meatballs and brown for 1 to 2 minutes. Shake the skillet to roll the meatballs in the oil. Transfer to a paper towel–lined plate to drain. Save 2 tablespoons of the frying oil.

8. In a large bowl, combine the reserved eggplants, reserved bell peppers, the garlic, lemon juice, sugar, salt, tomato paste, water, and the reserved oil and mix well.

9. Arrange the meatballs in one layer in a shallow ovenproof saucepan and pour over the sauce.

10. Bring to a boil on medium heat, cover, and transfer to the oven for 1 hour. Serve hot over rice or couscous.

KEBAB GEREZ | Meatballs with Sour Cherries

SYRIAN

I got this recipe from Pini Levi, an Israeli chef whose family comes from Urfa in Turkey, near the borders of Syria and Iraq. Believed to be the biblical Ur Kasdim, Abraham's birthplace, Urfa has been home for an ancient Jewish community with interesting cooking traditions. Among them are rich, strongly flavored dishes made with the local sour cherry fruit. This recipe is a great example; similar versions can be found in areas of Syria, notably in Aleppo. In season, use fresh pitted cherries; the rest of the year, preserved cherries would do. Make sure they are not preserved in heavy syrup, lest the dish be too sweet.

Serves 6

For the meatballs

1 large onion

1 pound ($\frac{1}{2}$ kg) finely ground beef

$\frac{1}{2}$ teaspoon freshly ground black pepper

$\frac{1}{2}$ teaspoon ground allspice

$\frac{1}{4}$ teaspoon ground cinnamon (optional)

Vegetable oil for frying

For the sauce

1 pound ($\frac{1}{2}$ kg) fresh cherries, pitted, or preserved sour cherries, drained

1 tablespoon dark brown sugar (optional; depends on sweetness of cherries)

$2\frac{1}{2}$ cups boiling water

1 cup semidry white wine, such as Gewürztraminer, Riesling, or Muscat

1 tablespoon white wine vinegar

1 cardamom pod, cracked (with the pod), or a dash of ground cardamom

Salt and freshly ground black pepper

1. **Prepare the meatballs** Grate the onion on a coarse grater. Squeeze out the excess liquid and transfer to a large bowl.

2. Add the meat, pepper, allspice, and cinnamon (if using). Knead thoroughly with your hands and refrigerate the mixture for 30 minutes.

3. **Prepare the sauce** Put half of the cherries in a wide medium saucepan. Add the brown sugar (if using), water, white wine, vinegar, and cardamom. Bring to a boil, reduce the heat, cover, and simmer for 20 to 25 minutes. Puree with an immersion blender or in a food processor until smooth. Taste and adjust the seasoning. Transfer to a medium saucepan and set aside.

4. Wet your hands or rub them with oil and form tiny meatballs (slightly bigger than the cherries).

5. Heat the vegetable oil in a large skillet. Add the meatballs and brown for 1 to 2 minutes. Shake the skillet to roll the meatballs in the oil. Transfer to a paper towel–lined plate to absorb the oil.

6. Carefully add the meatballs to the sauce. Add the rest of the cherries. At this point, the sauce should barely cover the contents of the pan. If it doesn't, add some more boiling water (up to $\frac{1}{2}$ cup). Cover and cook for 20 minutes. Serve over rice.

FESENJAN | Meatballs in Walnut and Pomegranate Sauce

PERSIAN

This recipe is from Rachel Norehlian, who owns a small restaurant called Gohar, in the town of Kfar Saba, one of the few in Israel to celebrate authentic Jewish Persian cuisine. Fesenjan can be made with lamb, chicken, or meatballs. What makes it unique is the sauce, based on ground walnuts, pomegranate syrup, honey, and ginger. It is favored by Persian Jews for important meals, especially on Rosh Hashanah, when pomegranates are in season and tradition calls for sweet dishes.

Serves 6 to 8

For the meatballs

1 onion

2 pounds (1 kg) ground beef

7 ounces (200 g) walnuts, finely chopped in a food processor (be careful not to grind them into a powder)

1 cup chopped fresh parsley

3 tablespoons good-quality bread crumbs

2 tablespoons extra virgin olive oil

1 teaspoon ground cumin

1 teaspoon freshly ground black pepper

Salt

For the sauce

3 tablespoons vegetable oil

1 medium onion, finely chopped

4 garlic cloves, finely chopped

1 tablespoon fresh ginger, finely chopped

10 ounces (300 g) walnuts, finely chopped in a food processor

2 cups boiling water

1 teaspoon salt

1 teaspoon freshly ground black pepper

$\frac{1}{2}$ cup date honey (silan; see page 147) or $\frac{1}{3}$ cup regular honey

$\frac{1}{2}$ cup pomegranate syrup (pomegranate molasses)

Fresh pomegranate seeds for garnish (optional)

1. Preheat the oven to 375°F (190°C). Line a large baking sheet with parchment.

2. **Prepare the meatballs** Grate the onion on a coarse grater, and squeeze out the excess liquid. Transfer to a large bowl.

3. Add the meat, walnuts, onion, parsley, bread crumbs, olive oil, cumin, pepper, and salt. Knead thoroughly with your hands.

4. Wet your hands or rub them with oil and form meatballs the size of a golf ball. Transfer to the baking sheet.

5. Bake the meatballs for 12 to 15 minutes, until they start to turn golden.

6. **Prepare the sauce** Heat the vegetable oil in a large wide saucepan over medium heat. Add the onion and sauté until golden. Add the garlic and ginger and sauté briefly, until fragrant. Add the ground walnuts and cook, stirring, for 2 to 3 minutes, until fragrant and golden brown.

7. Add the boiling water, salt, and pepper and bring to a boil. Reduce the heat to a gentle simmer, slide the meatballs into the pan, and return to a boil. Reduce the heat to the minimum, cover, and simmer for 1 hour. Add the date honey and pomegranate syrup and simmer for another 30 minutes. Taste and adjust the seasoning. Sprinkle with fresh pomegranate seeds (if using) and serve over rice.

HERBED FISH BALLS WITH JERUSALEM ARTICHOKES, TOMATOES, AND SAFFRON

MOROCCAN

So many goodies in one dish that is fun to cook and a pleasure to serve. Peeling Jerusalem artichokes (also called sunchokes) is a bit time-consuming, but the flavor of this vegetable is so lovely that it is worth the trouble. When they are in season, use fresh ripe tomatoes; the rest of the year, canned ones are a better alternative. In Jewish Moroccan homes, this dish is reserved for Friday-night dinners and special occasions.

Note: When peeling and cutting the Jerusalem artichokes, have a bowl of acidulated water ready and transfer the cut artichokes to it to prevent browning. Just before use, strain them and dry on paper towels.

Serves 6

For the fish balls

1 onion

1 pound (½ kg) meaty white fish, such as cod, tilapia, or halibut, finely chopped or minced

½ bunch fresh cilantro (mostly leaves), finely chopped

2 garlic cloves, crushed

1 egg

½ cup good-quality bread crumbs

1 teaspoon ground cumin

Salt and freshly ground black pepper

For the sauce

¼ cup olive oil

10 garlic cloves

2 onions, chopped

Salt

4 ripe tomatoes, diced, or one 14-ounce (400-g) can crushed tomatoes

3 celery stalks, coarsely chopped

½ bunch fresh cilantro (mostly stems), chopped

1 tablespoon ground cumin

1½ teaspoons sweet paprika

½ teaspoon cayenne pepper (optional)

2 pounds (1 kg) Jerusalem artichokes, peeled and cut into coarse chunks

2½ cups water

15 saffron threads, soaked in ½ cup lukewarm water

1. Prepare the fish balls Grate the onion on a coarse grater. Squeeze out the excess liquid and transfer to a large bowl.

2. Add the fish, cilantro, garlic, egg, bread crumbs, cumin, salt, and pepper. Knead thoroughly with your hands for a couple minutes. Refrigerate the mixture for 1 hour.

3. Prepare the sauce Pour the olive oil into a large wide pan and immediately add the garlic cloves. Sauté on medium heat only until fragrant, then add the onions. Season with salt and sauté for 5 minutes, until translucent.

4. Add the tomatoes and celery and sauté for 2 minutes. Add the cilantro, cumin, paprika, and cayenne (if using) and stir well. Add the Jerusalem artichokes and water, bring to a boil, and lower the heat. Add the saffron (with the liquid) and cook, partially covered, for 20 minutes.

5. Wet your hands or rub them with oil and form fish balls the size of a walnut. Slide the balls into the pan with the sauce, making sure they are submerged in the sauce (add more water, if necessary), and bring a boil. Reduce the heat, cover, and simmer for 30 minutes. Serve over couscous.

VARIATIONS

• Substitute 1 pound frozen quartered artichoke hearts for the Jerusalem artichokes.

• Substitute the same amount of ground chicken (I like combining dark and white chicken meat for extra juiciness) for the fish.

PEPPERS STUFFED WITH RICE AND MEAT

BULGARIAN

Naturally hollow, bell peppers are very easy to fill. So if you have never tried your hand at stuffing vegetables, this is a great recipe to start with. Before setting out, make sure you have a suitable pan, wide and shallow, that can hold all the peppers snugly in one layer, so they support each other. If your pan is too small, reduce the number of bell peppers. If it is a little too big, see Tips and Variations.

Makes 10 to 12 peppers

For the peppers

10 to 12 red and/or yellow bell peppers, uniformly sized

For the filling

3 tablespoons vegetable oil

2 medium onions

1 cup long-grain rice

10 ounces (300 g) ground beef

1 large tomato, grated
(see page 162)

⅓ cup fresh parsley leaves, chopped

1 teaspoon sweet paprika

Salt and freshly ground black pepper

½ cup pine nuts, toasted (optional)

For the sauce

¾ cup (150 g) tomato paste

1½ cups chicken or beef stock or water

3 to 4 garlic cloves, minced

1 teaspoon sugar

Salt and freshly ground black pepper

1. **Prepare the peppers** Cut off the tops of the bell peppers (with the stems) and set aside. Remove the white membranes and seeds and discard.

2. **Prepare the filling** Heat the vegetable oil in a skillet over medium heat. Add the onions and sauté until soft and golden. Add the rice and stir until the grains turn opaque. Add the meat and sauté, crumbling it with a fork, until it changes color. Stir in the grated tomato, parsley, paprika, salt, black pepper, and pine nuts (if using). Remove from the heat and cool for a few minutes.

3. Stuff the bell peppers to three-quarters of their capacity (rice swells during cooking).

4. **Prepare the sauce** Dilute the tomato paste in the stock. Add the garlic, sugar, salt, and black pepper and bring to a boil in a large wide pan that can hold all the peppers in one layer. Pour off ½ cup of the sauce and set aside.

5. Arrange the peppers, open side up, snugly in the pan in one layer—they should prevent one another from tipping over. Spoon the reserved sauce over the filling.

6. Bring to a boil, cover with a tight-fitting lid, reduce the heat, and simmer for 1½ hours. Occasionally check that there is some liquid left in the bottom of the pan (the peppers don't need to be submerged in the sauce). Carefully pour in a little stock, if necessary. Let stand for 15 minutes before serving.

TIPS AND VARIATIONS

• Sometimes after you arrange the bell peppers in the pan, there is a gap left because the pan is slightly too wide. Fill it with a whole tomato or whole peeled onion—it will soften during cooking and add flavor to the sauce.

• For a prettier presentation, cook the bell peppers with their caps and stems. To do this, cut off the caps, making sure the stems remain attached. Remove the seeds and membranes from the cavities, stuff the peppers, spoon some sauce onto the filling, and replace the caps. Cook as directed.

• **FOR A MEATLESS VERSION** Sauté 3 onions until golden, add 1½ cups rice, and stir until opaque. Add 2 grated tomatoes, 3 tablespoons chopped fresh parsley, 3 tablespoons chopped fresh dill, and ½ cup toasted pine nuts. Season generously with salt, black pepper, sweet paprika, and a dash of cumin. Stuff the peppers to two-thirds of their capacity. Cook as directed.

MEATBALLS WITH TOMATOES, CHICKPEAS, SWISS CHARD, AND EGGPLANTS

ISRAELI

This is one of the few recipes in this book that were actually born in my kitchen. Inspired by several ethnic dishes and featuring some of my favorite ingredients, it is pretty close in spirit to Sephardic albondigas (see page 60).

Serves 6

For the meatballs

1 onion

1 pound (½ kg) ground beef
(or a combination of ground beef
and ground chicken)

1 egg

2 to 3 tablespoons good-quality
bread crumbs

⅓ cup fresh cilantro or parsley
leaves, finely chopped

1 teaspoon baharat spice mix
(page 150 or store-bought)

Salt and freshly ground black pepper

For the sauce

1 large eggplant, cut into 1-inch
(2½-cm) cubes

½ cup extra virgin olive oil

1 tablespoon coarse salt

4 to 5 garlic cloves, thinly sliced

Two 14-ounce (400-g) cans crushed
tomatoes

1 cup chicken stock, water, or
vegetable juice, such as V8

1 teaspoon baharat spice mix
(page 150 or store-bought)

1 teaspoon sugar

1 cup cooked or canned chickpeas

Salt and freshly ground black pepper

1 bunch Swiss chard, leaves only,
coarsely chopped

1. **Prepare the meatballs** Grate the onion on a coarse grater. Squeeze out the excess liquid and transfer to a large bowl.

2. Add the meat, egg, bread crumbs, cilantro, baharat, salt, and pepper. Knead thoroughly with your hands and refrigerate the mixture for 30 minutes.

3. Preheat the oven to 400°F (200°C).

4. **Prepare the sauce** Arrange the cubed eggplant on a parchment-lined baking sheet. Drizzle with ¼ cup of the olive oil, sprinkle the coarse salt, and bake for 30 minutes, until golden brown.

5. Pour the remaining ¼ cup oil into a large wide saucepan. Add the garlic and sauté for 1 minute, only until fragrant. Add the canned tomatoes, chicken stock, baharat, and sugar. Bring to a boil, reduce the heat, and simmer for 10 to 15 minutes. Don't add more salt yet because roasted eggplants are quite salty.

6. Add the roasted eggplants and chickpeas and simmer for another 5 minutes. Taste and adjust the seasoning with salt and pepper.

7. Wet your hands or rub them with oil and form meatballs the size of a walnut. Slide the meatballs into the simmering sauce. The meatballs should be submerged in the sauce. If they are not, add more stock.

8. Arrange the chopped Swiss chard on top of the meatballs—don't stir so as not to disturb the meatballs. During cooking, the chard will wilt and become part of the sauce. Cover and simmer for 30 minutes. Serve over couscous, rice, or mashed potatoes.

STUFFED CABBAGE ROLLS WITH SAUERKRAUT

HUNGARIAN

Holishkes in Yiddish, golubtzi in Russian, golabki in Polish: Stuffed cabbage rolls are ubiquitous across Eastern Europe. But the Hungarian version, called töltött káposzta, is the most intriguing with its peppery seasoning and sauerkraut-based sauce. Look for cabbages that are relatively lightweight for their size—their leaves separate more easily.

Serves 8

For the cabbage rolls

1 large head green cabbage

For the filling

2 onions

½ cup long-grain rice

1 pound (½ kg) ground beef

3 garlic cloves, crushed

1 cup water

1 tablespoon salt

1 teaspoon freshly ground black pepper

1 tablespoon sweet Hungarian paprika

For the sauce

3 tablespoons vegetable oil

3 garlic cloves, chopped

1 teaspoon salt

½ teaspoon freshly ground black pepper

1 tablespoon sweet Hungarian paprika

1 teaspoon sugar

½ teaspoon chili powder

½ head (about 1½ pounds) green cabbage, chopped

One 14-ounce (400-g) can sauerkraut, rinsed and strained

2 cups tomato juice

1 cup water

1. **Prepare the cabbage rolls** Fill a large pot with water until it is three-quarters full and bring to a boil. With a sharp knife, cut a deep and narrow cone at the base of the green cabbage, pull out the core, and discard it.

2. Transfer the cabbage (without the core) to the boiling water, base (cut) side down. Cook, covered, for 15 minutes, until the leaves separate easily. Remove from the pot and set aside any leaves that fall off. Transfer the whole cabbage to a large tray or a cutting board (the easiest way to pick up the hot cabbage is with two large spoons).

3. Separate the leaves with tongs and a fork. Don't worry if the leaves tear slightly. Place the leaves in a pile in a strainer, concave side up.

4. **Prepare the filling** Grate the onions on a coarse grater and squeeze out the excess liquid. Transfer to a large bowl. Add the rice, meat, garlic, water, salt, pepper, and paprika and mix well.

5. Trim off the tough outer spine of a large cabbage leaf and discard it. Place the leaf on a table, veiny side down.

6. Put a heaping tablespoon of filling in the center of the leaf. Roll the bottom part of the leaf halfway to cover the filling. Fold in the edges from right and left over the folded flap and loosely roll (rice swells during cooking, and if the roll is too tight it might tear). Prepare the rest of the rolls the same way.

7. **Prepare the sauce** Heat the vegetable oil in a large wide saucepan over medium heat. Add the garlic, salt, pepper, paprika, sugar, and chili powder and sauté for 1 minute, until fragrant. Remove from the heat.

8. Add the chopped green cabbage and the sauerkraut. Pour over the tomato juice and water and return to the heat. Bring to a boil, lower the heat, and cook for about 5 minutes. Taste and adjust the seasoning.

9. Arrange the cabbage rolls, seam side down, in one snug layer in the saucepan. Make sure the rolls are submerged in the sauce. Add a little bit of tomato juice or water, if necessary.

10. Bring to a boil, cover, and simmer over very low heat for 1 to 1½ hours, until the liquid has reduced by half. Serve hot.

VARIATION

- **FOR A MEATLESS VERSION** Increase the rice amount to 1 cup. Finely chop 4 onions and sauté them over medium heat with some salt and pepper until soft and golden brown, about 10 minutes. Add 1 tablespoon caraway seeds and sauté for 2 more minutes. Season with freshly ground black pepper. Add the onion mixture to the rice instead of meat and proceed with the recipe. Serve with a generous dollop of sour cream.

MIXED STUFFED VEGETABLES IN POMEGRANATE SAUCE

SYRIAN (ALEPPAN)

This, in my opinion, is the grand slam of stuffed vegetable dishes. The sauce, made with pomegranate juice and prunes (or dried apricots) and perfumed with mint and allspice, is reduced by the end of cooking to a thick syrup that glazes the vegetables and begs to be wiped off the plate with a piece of bread. The classic casserole is prepared with three different vegetables (onions, zucchini, and eggplants), but you can use only one, if you wish.

Serves 6 to 8

For the filling

1 onion

1 pound (½ kg) ground beef

½ cup long-grain rice

½ bunch fresh mint leaves, finely chopped

Salt and freshly ground black pepper

½ teaspoon ground allspice

1 teaspoon dried mint

2 to 3 tablespoons vegetable or olive oil

¼ cup fresh lemon juice

For the vegetables

10 to 12 very small zucchini

5 small eggplants, such as fairy tale, bambino, or young Chinese eggplants

3 to 4 large onions

3 to 4 tablespoons vegetable or olive oil

4 garlic cloves, chopped

12 prunes or dried apricots

½ bunch mint sprigs

½ cup fresh lemon juice

For the sauce

3 tablespoons pomegranate syrup (pomegranate molasses)

Salt and freshly ground black pepper

2 tablespoons honey or sugar

2 cups pomegranate juice

8 to 10 fresh mint sprigs

1. Prepare the filling Grate the onion on a coarse grater. Squeeze out the excess liquid and transfer to a large bowl.

2. Add the meat, rice, fresh mint, salt, pepper, allspice, dried mint, vegetable oil, and lemon juice and mix well. Refrigerate for 30 minutes.

3. Prepare the vegetables for stuffing Cut off the ends of the zucchini. Using an apple corer and working from the bottom end, hollow them by creating a tunnel at the center. Leave about ¼ inch (⅓ cm) of flesh along the interior walls. Repeat with the eggplants, but leave the stems intact.

4. Cut a deep X across the tops of the onions, starting at the stem end and working toward the root end. Heat for 4 to 5 minutes in the microwave at full power or blanch in boiling water for 3 to 4 minutes to soften. Cool slightly. When the onions are cool enough to handle, remove 4 or 5 of the largest outer layers and set aside.

5. Stuff the centers of the zucchini and eggplants gently with the meat filling, without compressing (you can use a teaspoon, but I find working with fingers to be easier).

6. To stuff the onion layers, hold 1 layer with the curved side cupped in your hand. Spoon 1 to 2 tablespoons of stuffing into the center and gently fold over to form a football-shaped packet. Repeat with the rest of the layers.

7. Pour the vegetable oil into a large wide pan that can hold all the vegetables in one layer. Add the garlic and arrange the stuffed vegetables in a single layer (onion packets, seam-side down). Arrange the prunes between the vegetables. Place the ½ bunch mint sprigs on top.

8. Prepare the sauce Combine the pomegranate syrup, salt, pepper, honey, pomegranate juice, and 8 to 10 mint sprigs in a bowl and mix well. Gently pour over the vegetables and bring to a boil. Cover and simmer over low heat for about 1 hour. Drizzle on the lemon juice and continue cooking for up to 2 hours, until the sauce is syrupy and the vegetables are very soft. If the vegetables are ready but the sauce is still too runny, increase the heat and cook, uncovered, for 10 to 15 minutes to reduce.

9. Let rest for 20 minutes before serving. The casserole can be reheated over low heat (add a bit of pomegranate juice or water to avoid scorching).

MAFROUM | Meat and Potato "Sandwiches"

LIBYAN (TRIPOLITAN)

N o need to hollow out or roll anything here. Just slit potato slices crosswise so they resemble a crocodile's mouth and stuff with a meat patty. Mafroum is traditionally served over couscous, but you can serve it over white rice or on its own (in which case, lots of bread to mop up the sauce is imperative). This recipe is from Rafi Guetta, chef-owner of Guetta restaurant in Jaffa, one of the best places in Israel to savor Libyan (Tripolitan) cuisine.

Makes 10 to 12 mafroum; serves 4 to 6

For the filling

1 pound (½ kg) coarsely ground beef

½ pound (250 g) coarsely ground chicken breast

1 large onion, finely chopped

⅓ cup fresh parsley leaves, finely chopped

For the mafroum

4 russet potatoes, peeled

½ cup unbleached all-purpose flour

2 eggs

1 teaspoon salt

½ teaspoon freshly ground black pepper

½ cup good-quality (preferably homemade or panko) bread crumbs

Vegetable oil for frying

For the sauce

Olive oil

Leftover potato scraps

1 large onion, thinly sliced

1 carrot, sliced into ½-inch (¾-cm) coins

1 teaspoon sweet paprika

½ teaspoon sugar

2 tablespoons tomato paste

Salt and freshly ground black pepper

½ to 1 teaspoon ground cinnamon (optional)

1. Prepare the filling Combine the beef, chicken, onion, and parsley in a bowl and mix well. Form 10 to 12 round flat patties 2 inches (5 centimeters) in diameter.

2. Prepare the mafroum Slice the potatoes lengthwise into 1-inch (2½-cm) disks. Reserve the scraps for later use. Slit each disk, but not all the way through, so the sides can be hinged to create a V shape to be filled (see the photograph). Insert the meat patty into the opening.

3. Prepare three plates: one with the flour, one with the beaten eggs seasoned with the salt and pepper, and one with the bread crumbs. Dip the potato sandwiches first in the flour, then in the eggs, and finally in the bread crumbs.

4. Heat the vegetable oil in a wide shallow saucepan and fry the potato sandwiches for 2 to 3 minutes on each side until golden. Transfer to a paper towel–lined plate.

5. Prepare the sauce Heat the olive oil in a large wide pan over medium heat. Add the leftover potato scraps and sauté until golden. Add the onion, carrot, paprika, sugar, and tomato paste and sauté until the onion softens and becomes translucent, 2 to 3 minutes.

6. Arrange the potato sandwiches in an even layer over the sauce and pour water over just to cover. Season with salt, pepper, and cinnamon (if using) and bring to a boil. Reduce the heat, cover, and simmer for 45 minutes, or until the potatoes are very tender.

VARIATION

To make mafroum kosher for Passover, dip the sandwiches in potato starch instead of flour and then in the eggs. Skip the bread crumbs.

BISTIL | Potato Patties Stuffed with Spiced Minced Meat

LIBYAN (TRIPOLITAN)

This dish of golden mashed potato patties stuffed with aromatics tastes even better than it sounds. It is common among Jewish Libyan families to serve bistil at the Seder table. Be warned: Bistil taste and smell so good when coming out of the pan that there is a risk they will be gone before the guests arrive.

Makes 20 bistil; serves 8 to 10

For the filling

2 tablespoons vegetable oil

1 onion, chopped

1 pound (½ kg) beef shoulder or brisket in one piece

1 teaspoon salt

1 teaspoon freshly ground black pepper

2 allspice berries

2 bay leaves

¼ teaspoon ground nutmeg

For the shell

2½ pounds (about 1 kg) russet potatoes, unpeeled

1 teaspoon white pepper

1 teaspoon ground turmeric

3 egg yolks

Salt

1 teaspoon ras el hanout (see page 51) or baharat spice mix (see page 150)

For frying

½ cup unbleached all-purpose flour (or potato starch for Passover)

2 eggs, lightly beaten

Vegetable oil

1. **Prepare the filling** Heat the vegetable oil in a pan over medium heat. Add the onion and sauté for 7 to 8 minutes, until golden. Add the meat and brown on all sides. Add the salt, black pepper, allspice, bay leaves, and nutmeg and cook for a few more minutes.

2. Add water to cover and bring to a boil. Cover the pan, lower the heat, and simmer for about 1½ hours, until the meat is tender. Remove the meat and onion from the pan to cool.

3. Grind the seasoned meat and onion in a meat grinder or finely chop with a large sharp knife. Set aside.

4. **Prepare the shell** Meanwhile, bring the potatoes to a boil in plenty of salted water. Cook until fork tender (about 30 minutes after the water comes to a boil). Drain and cool.

5. Peel the potatoes and place in a bowl. Mash with a potato masher or a fork; do not use a food processor. Add the white pepper, turmeric, egg yolks, salt, and ras el hanout and mix until just blended—be careful, because overmixing will hurt the texture.

6. **Shape, fill, and fry** Wet your hands or rub them with oil and form the potato mixture into balls 2 inches (5 cm) in diameter, snuggling them in the palm of your hand. Flatten them slightly. Place 1 tablespoon of the filling in the center of each patty and pinch over so the filling is completely covered with mashed potatoes and you have formed an oblong patty.

7. Prepare two plates: one with the flour and one with the beaten eggs. Dip the patties in the flour, then in the beaten eggs.

8. Heat the vegetable oil in a large wide pan (the oil should come halfway up the sides of the patties). Working in batches, fry the patties for 2 to 3 minutes on each side until lightly golden. Transfer to a paper towel–lined plate.

9. Serve immediately or keep in a 300°F (150°C) oven until ready to serve. Serve hot or at room temperature.

VARIATION

Instead of using the spice mix (baharat or ras el hanout), use a dash each of black pepper, allspice, cumin, nutmeg, and cinnamon.

Braises, Pot Roasts, and Ragùs

Slow, gentle cooking renders inexpensive cuts of meat fork tender and transforms ordinary chicken into a succulent delicacy; it infuses cooking liquids with meaty aromas and thickens them into sauces that beg to be wiped off the plate with a piece of bread. Time is the secret ingredient in this chapter. Whether it's Hungarian beef goulash or Moroccan chicken tagine, the longer you cook it, the better it tastes.

BEEF AND POTATO SOFRITO

SEPHARDIC

For Sephardic Jews who descend from the Balkans, this casserole evokes memories of Friday-night dinners. The term sofrito does not refer to a specific dish but rather to a technique: First, potatoes are briefly deep-fried and then added to a pot where beef or chicken has been slowly braising. The result is a golden-brown pot roast with meltingly tender meat and potatoes that have retained their shape despite the lengthy cooking.

Apparently not just Sephardic Jews yearn for food cooked this way. For many years, I have been trying to re-create my grandmother Rosa's zharkoye ("pot roast" in Russian). I prepared a few recipes by the same name, but none came close, until I made a sofrito. It had that juicy yet crispy texture and the deep flavors I was looking for. Rosa was a native of Bessarabia (a province of Romania), and her cooking, though formally Ashkenazi, was strongly influenced by the Balkans. Who knows? Perhaps it was sofrito I was looking for all these years.

Note: Authentic sofrito calls for deep-frying the potatoes, but I found that roasting them produces almost identical results with much less oil involved.

Serves 6 to 8

⅓ cup vegetable oil

2 pounds (1 kg) stewing beef, such as chuck or brisket, sliced or cut into 1-inch (2½-cm) cubes

Salt and freshly ground black pepper

Dash of ground turmeric or sweet paprika

1 head garlic, halved

½ cup boiling water, or more if needed

10 red or Yukon Gold potatoes, peeled and cut into wedges

1. Heat half of the oil in a large heavy pot or casserole over medium-high heat. Add the meat and brown on all sides. Season with salt, pepper, and turmeric.

2. Add the garlic and boiling water, cover with a tight-fitting lid, reduce the heat to the minimum, and cook for 2 hours. Add a bit of water if the liquid in the pot dries out. The idea is to cook the dish in as little liquid as possible.

3. While the meat is cooking, preheat the oven to 400°F (200°C).

4. Arrange the potato wedges on a baking sheet, drizzle with the remaining oil, and sprinkle with salt and pepper.

5. Roast for 15 minutes, until the potatoes are golden and crisp on the outside and partially cooked inside.

6. Add the potato wedges to the pot with the meat (after it has cooked for about 2 hours). Cover and simmer on the lowest heat for another hour.

VARIATIONS

- **CHICKEN SOFRITO** Substitute 10 chicken thighs and/or drumsticks for the beef.

- Substitute the same amount of unpeeled fingerlings or other very small potatoes for the potato wedges.

- Add 6 to 8 very small, whole peeled onions together with the meat.

- Add 2 teaspoons baharat spice mix (see page 150) with the salt and pepper.

- As a homage to my grandmother's zharkoye, I sometimes add 10 to 12 prunes to the casserole along with the liquids.

BARBECUED BRISKET

AMERICAN

I became aware of brisket and its iconic status in the Jewish culinary world while leading a group of Jewish American and Canadian food writers on a culinary tour of Israel. Members of this tightly knit and opinionated group asked time and again about brisket and its role in the local food scene. To my embarrassment, I was a bit vague as to what exactly a brisket was. In Israel we do have something called tzli (literally, a "roast"). It is usually braised, sliced, and served in nondescript gravy at low-budget wedding receptions.

After looking into this matter, I discovered that (a) brisket is the name of a cut that doesn't formally exist in the Israeli butchering system; (b) it became part of the Jewish cooking tradition in North America in the early twentieth century; (c) it can be either braised or barbecued; and (d) it is much better than the Israeli tzli.

Bonnie Stern, a wonderful Canadian cookbook author, was kind enough to contribute her favorite barbecued brisket recipe to this collection.

Serves 12 to 16

For the brisket

2 tablespoons smoked paprika

1 tablespoon coarse salt

¼ cup firmly packed dark brown sugar

1 tablespoon ground cumin

1 tablespoon garlic powder

1 whole brisket (about 8 pounds/ 3½ kg)

For the barbecue sauce

1½ cups of your favorite store-bought barbecue sauce or ketchup

1 cup beer or water

¼ cup maple syrup or honey

¼ cup firmly packed dark brown sugar

2 tablespoons Dijon mustard

2 tablespoons Worcestershire sauce

2 tablespoons cider vinegar

1 tablespoon chipotle puree or chipotle Tabasco sauce (available at spice and specialty stores and some supermarkets) or 1 teaspoon Tabasco sauce

3 large onions, thinly sliced

1 head garlic, broken into cloves and peeled

1. Prepare the brisket Combine the paprika, salt, brown sugar, cumin, and garlic powder in a bowl. Pat the rub into both sides of the brisket. Place in a large nonreactive bowl or on a baking sheet, cover, and marinate in the refrigerator for up to 8 hours (or cook right away).

2. Preheat the oven to 325°F (160°C).

3. Prepare the barbecue sauce Combine the barbecue sauce, beer, maple syrup, brown sugar, mustard, Worcestershire sauce, vinegar, and chipotle puree in a medium bowl.

4. Place the onions and garlic on the bottom of a large Dutch oven or a deep roasting pan. Place the brisket, fat side up, on the onions. Pour on the barbecue sauce. There should be about 1 inch of liquid in the pan. Add water, if necessary. Cover the surface of the brisket with parchment. Bring to a boil on top of the stove, cover tightly, and place in the oven.

5. Braise for 4 to 6 hours. The brisket should be completely tender when pierced with a fork. Check every 45 minutes and add more water, if necessary. If the top has not browned, remove the cover and paper and return to the oven for 15 to 20 minutes.

6. Remove the brisket to a carving board and pour the juices into a large cup or bowl. Let cool and discard the fat that separates from the top. Carve the brisket and serve with the juices.

MAKING AHEAD

Remove the cooked meat from the juices and refrigerate each in a separate container. Remove the fat that solidifies over the juices. To reheat: Preheat the oven to 325°F (160°C). Slice the brisket thinly, arrange in overlapping slices in a large baking pan, and pour over the juices (you will need 2 to 3 cups; add water, if necessary). Cover the pan tightly and heat for 45 minutes until very hot.

GOULASH | Beef Stewed in Paprika Sauce

HUNGARIAN

Brought to Israel by Jewish Hungarian immigrants, goulash has gained such popularity in its new home that it has become synonymous with any beef casserole in a piquant red sauce. When shopping for stewing meat Israelis would casually ask the butcher for "goulash meat." Here, however, is the real thing—a recipe I learned from Avi Steinitz, a friend and a terrific chef. I make it exactly the way he taught me at least once a month, especially during winter.

Avi's number one secret for a great goulash is onions, lots of them. This recipe calls for an equal amount of onions and meat! During cooking, the onions lose their sharpness and dissolve into a deliciously thick sauce. Equally important is the use of a good-quality paprika (preferably Hungarian) that enhances both flavor and color. And please don't omit the caraway—it is crucial for that elusive authentic touch.

Serves 6 to 8

3 tablespoons schmaltz (goose or chicken fat, see page 14) or vegetable oil

2 pounds (1 kg) onions, sliced

1½ tablespoons best-quality sweet Hungarian paprika

2 pounds (1 kg) stewing beef, such as chuck or brisket, cut into 2-inch (5-cm) cubes

2 tablespoons tomato paste

6 garlic cloves, minced

1 tablespoon chopped fresh marjoram or 1 teaspoon dried marjoram (optional)

Salt and freshly ground black pepper

⅓ teaspoon ground caraway or ½ teaspoon whole caraway seeds

Pinch of hot paprika or cayenne pepper (optional)

2 to 3 cups chicken or beef stock or water

1. Heat the fat in a heavy-bottomed pot over medium heat. Add the onions and sauté until golden brown, about 10 minutes. Add the sweet paprika and stir briefly. Add the meat and brown on all sides.

2. Add the tomato paste and cook for 2 minutes. Add the garlic, marjoram (if using), salt, pepper, caraway, and hot paprika (if using) and mix well. Pour in the stock.

3. Bring to a boil, lower the heat, cover, and simmer for 2 to 3 hours, until the meat is very tender. Taste and adjust the seasoning.

VARIATION

GOULASH WITH POTATOES Follow the recipe, but after 1 hour and 20 minutes, add 4 to 6 potatoes, peeled and cut into large cubes. Boost the seasoning because the potatoes will absorb the flavors. Continue to cook as directed.

PLAU B'JEEJ | Chicken with Almonds and Raisins over Red Rice

IRAQI

First the chicken is cooked in water, tomato paste, and spices, then the spiced cooking liquid is used to make delicious red rice. Clever, huh? And there is more: While the rice is cooking, the chicken is shredded; slowly sautéed with onions, almonds, and raisins; and then served over the rice. Grandma's cooking at its best! Save any leftover red rice—it makes a delicious side for beef, chicken, and fish dishes.

Serves 4 to 6

4 chicken legs (thighs and drumsticks)

5 cups water

7 ounces (200 g) tomato paste

1 teaspoon ground cumin

1 teaspoon sweet paprika

Pinch of hot paprika or cayenne pepper (optional)

Salt

2 cups long-grain white rice

3 tablespoons vegetable oil

3 large onions, thinly sliced

Pinch of hot paprika or ground turmeric (optional)

1 teaspoon baharat spice mix (page 150 or store-bought)

½ cup blanched almonds (halved or slivered)

½ cup golden raisins

For garnish (optional)

1 tablespoon vegetable oil

⅓ cup blanched almonds (halved or slivered)

1. Place the chicken legs in a medium saucepan. Mix the water, tomato paste, cumin, paprika, and cayenne (if using) in a bowl. Pour over the chicken. Partially cover, bring to a boil, and simmer for about 1 hour over low heat until the chicken is tender. Toward the end of cooking, taste and season with salt.

2. While the chicken is cooking, soak the rice in water for 15 minutes. Rinse in cold water several times until the water runs clear. Drain in a colander.

3. Remove the cooked chicken to a plate with a slotted spoon and set aside to cool. Measure 3½ cups of hot cooking liquid and return it to the saucepan. Add 1 heaping teaspoon salt. Add the rice and bring to a boil. Lower the heat, cover tightly, and simmer over low heat for 20 minutes. Open the lid, fluff the rice with a fork, cover, and let stand for 5 to 10 minutes.

4. While the rice is cooking, heat the vegetable oil in a large shallow saucepan. Add the sliced onions and sauté over medium-low heat until soft and golden, at least 10 minutes. Season with salt, a dash of turmeric (if using), and the baharat.

5. When the chicken is cooled enough to be handled with bare hands, remove and discard the skin and the bones. Shred the meat into small pieces and add to the onions. Add the almonds and sauté for 5 to 6 minutes over medium heat. Add the raisins and sauté for another minute.

6. **Prepare the garnish (if using)** Heat the vegetable oil in a small frying pan and toss the almonds until golden and crisp. To serve, mound the chicken and onion mixture over the rice and garnish with toasted almonds.

USHPALAU | Beef and Rice Pilaf with Chickpeas, Carrots, and Spices

BUKHARAN

W ithout speaking a word in Hebrew, with only smiles and the international language of food, a group of Bukharan women cooked us ushpalau as prepared by their grandmothers—without weights, without measurements, a handful of this and a dash of that . . ." This is how Ruth Oliver described her first encounter with this wonderful dish during a workshop on traditional Bukharan cooking. Ushpalau (or plov) is indeed delightful, laden with goodies (beef, garlic, rice, chickpeas, and spices), while oodles of carrots add hints of sweetness and golden color to the rice.

You'll need only a bit of the spice mixture; store the rest in an airtight container and use it to flavor rice and meat dishes.

Serves 10

For the spice mixture

2 tablespoons cumin seeds, toasted

2 tablespoons coriander seeds, toasted

2 tablespoons black peppercorns

1 tablespoon chili powder

For the pilaf

3 cups short-grain rice

Salt

¼ cup vegetable oil, or more if needed

3 pounds (1½ kg) stewing beef, such as chuck or brisket, cut into 1-inch (2½-cm) cubes

2 large onions, sliced

2 pounds (1 kg) carrots, cut into matchsticks or coarsely shredded on a grater

1 to 2 heads garlic, tops and bottoms sliced off

1 cup cooked chickpeas (or canned or frozen)

1. Prepare the spice mixture Crush the cumin seeds, coriander seeds, peppercorns, and chili powder in a mortar and pestle or in a grinder.

2. Prepare the pilaf Soak the rice in a large bowl with 1 teaspoon salt and boiling water to cover for about 15 minutes. Rinse well in cold water several times until the water runs clear. Drain in a colander.

3. Heat the vegetable oil in a frying pan over medium-high heat. Add the cubes of meat and brown until they change color (work in batches, if necessary). Transfer to a medium pot with a little of the frying oil.

4. Sauté the onions in the frying pan with the remaining oil until they begin to soften. Remove from the pan and arrange over the meat.

5. Pour ½ cup water over onions and cook over low heat for 30 minutes. Arrange the carrots and the garlic over the meat. Spread the chickpeas over the carrots and sprinkle with 1 tablespoon of the spice mixture and 1½ teaspoons salt. Cover, reduce the heat to the minimum, and cook for another 30 minutes.

6. Add the drained rice to the pot and season with an additional 1 tablespoon of the spice mixture. Gently ladle or spoon boiling water over until it reaches 1 inch (2½ cm) above the rice (ladling or spooning will distribute the water evenly without disturbing the layers). Using the handle of a wooden spoon, form several "chimney" holes through the rice down to the bottom of the pot. Add a generous pinch of salt and bring to a boil. Cover with a tight-fitting lid and simmer on the lowest heat for 35 minutes. Set aside for about 10 minutes.

7. To serve, either flip the contents of the pot onto a large platter to preserve the layers or arrange the contents (rice, vegetables, meat) on a large platter.

VARIATIONS

- Sprinkle with 1 cup pomegranate seeds before serving.
- Substitute 10 to 12 chicken drumsticks for the beef.

CHICKEN TAGINE WITH ARTICHOKE HEARTS

MOROCCAN

The term "tagine" refers to a family of North African braises as well as to the pot in which they are cooked—an earthenware casserole with a wide bottom and a conical lid that creates a unique steaming effect. If you don't own a tagine, any heavy-bottomed casserole or a Dutch oven will do nicely. Most tagines combine protein (beef, lamb, fish, chicken) with seasonal vegetables. This one, based on artichokes, is traditionally served in spring and is especially popular with Jewish Moroccan families who often serve it for Passover. It is perfectly fine to use frozen artichoke hearts rather than spending a long time peeling fresh ones. However, I strongly advise not skipping the spices, which transform this easy-to-make chicken pot roast into an exotically flavored delicacy.

Serves 6 to 8

⅓ cup olive oil

10 to 12 chicken thighs and/or drumsticks

4 large onions, chopped

1 large bunch fresh parsley or cilantro, chopped

12 to 14 artichoke hearts, thickly sliced (if you are using frozen, thaw them first)

3 pickled (Moroccan) lemons, chopped or sliced (available at gourmet stores and Middle Eastern groceries; see Mail Order Sources, page 203, or homemade, see page 2)

2 cups cooked chickpeas (or canned or frozen)

1 teaspoon ground coriander

¼ teaspoon ground cumin

Dash of nutmeg (preferably freshly grated)

½ teaspoon ground turmeric

Salt and freshly ground black pepper

1 tablespoon sweet paprika

1. Heat half of the olive oil in a frying pan over medium-high heat. Add the chicken and brown for 3 to 4 minutes on each side. Add ⅓ cup water, cover, and simmer for 20 minutes, or until the chicken is almost done.

2. Heat the remaining oil in a tagine or in a large heavy-bottomed casserole. Add the onions and parsley and sauté until the onions are translucent, about 5 minutes. Add the artichokes and pickled lemons and sauté for 1 more minute. Add the chicken, chickpeas, coriander, cumin, nutmeg, turmeric, salt, pepper, and paprika. Pour in ⅓ cup boiling water. Reduce the heat to the minimum, cover, and simmer for 1 hour, gently stirring or shaking the pot occasionally. If the dish dries out (it shouldn't because the vegetables will release enough liquid), add a little bit of boiling water. After an hour or so, the tagine is ready, but if you have time, let it simmer gently for another hour or even more. The longer you cook it, the better the taste, and the more succulent the chicken will be. Serve over couscous.

TANZIYE | Beef Tagine with Dried Fruits and Nuts

MOROCCAN

Tanziye is a mélange of dried fruits and nuts soaked and cooked in wine, honey, and spices and served over couscous. When meat is added (chicken, beef, or lamb chops), the result is a casserole fit for a feast, especially for Rosh Hashanah, when it is customary to eat sweet dishes.

Serves 6 to 8

5 dried figs

15 dried apricots

15 prunes, pitted

1 cup raisins

1½ cups dry red wine

2 pounds (1 kg) stewing beef, such as chuck or brisket, cut into 2-inch (5-cm) cubes

Salt and freshly ground black pepper

¼ cup olive oil

4 large onions, thinly sliced

2 tablespoons honey

1 teaspoon ground coriander

2 cinnamon sticks or 1 teaspoon ground cinnamon

¼ teaspoon ground cardamom

1 teaspoon ground turmeric

1 teaspoon ground cumin

1 inch (2½ cm) fresh ginger, peeled and grated

3 tablespoons fresh lemon juice

½ cup walnut halves

½ cup blanched almonds

⅓ cup pine nuts

2 oranges, peeled and sliced crosswise (optional)

1. In a large bowl, soak the figs, apricots, prunes, and raisins in the red wine for 1 hour.

2. Put the meat in a medium pot, add water to cover, season with salt and pepper, and bring to a boil. Skim the foam off the surface, reduce the heat, cover, and simmer for 1 hour until the meat is almost fork tender. Drain and reserve about 1 cup of the cooking liquid.

3. Heat the olive oil in a tagine or a large heavy-bottomed casserole. Add the onions and sauté until translucent, about 5 minutes. Add the honey and cook for another 8 minutes, until deep golden. Add the meat to the pan. Drain the dried fruit (reserve the wine) and add to the casserole.

4. Add the coriander, cinnamon, cardamom, turmeric, cumin, salt, and pepper and mix well. Cook for 5 to 6 minutes. Add the reserved wine, ginger, and lemon juice. Taste and adjust the seasoning.

5. Reduce the heat to the minimum, cover, and simmer for 30 minutes, or until the meat is tender. Stir or shake the pan occasionally to make sure the meat doesn't stick to the bottom. Only if the liquid in the pot dries out, add a little bit of the reserved cooking liquid, ¼ cup at a time.

6. Heat a frying pan (without oil) over medium heat. Toast the walnuts, almonds, and pine nuts separately until golden. Add the nuts to the casserole, toss gently, and turn off the heat. Garnish with sliced oranges (if using) and serve with couscous.

SALONA | Sweet-and-Sour Fish Casserole with Eggplant and Tomatoes

IRAQI

Similar to Ingriyi (page 94) in flavors and technique, salona has many variations. I've always made it with eggplant and tomatoes, but while researching recipes for this book, I discovered other versions of this famous Jewish Iraqi fish casserole. Some contain only tomatoes; some are cooked on the stove, while others are baked in the oven; in some cases fish fillets are breaded before they are fried, while in others they are not. The only constant is the sweet-and-sour sauce—the hallmark of Jewish Iraqi cuisine. I like the following version because it is hassle free and light: Fish fillets are briefly fried just to add a bit of crispness and flavor, and the layered casserole is baked in the oven. Yes, there is eggplant, because it is so delicious when it absorbs cooking juices. If you don't like eggplant, you can leave it out and still have an authentic salona.

Serves 4 to 6

1 eggplant, peeled and sliced lengthwise into ½-inch (1½-cm)-thick slices

⅓ cup olive oil

Coarse salt

3 to 4 onions, cut into ⅓-inch (1-cm) slices

4 to 5 firm, ripe tomatoes, cut into ⅓-inch (1-cm) slices

1 pound (500 g) white fish fillets, such as cod, halibut, or tilapia, skin on, cut into portion-size chunks

¼ fresh hot green chile pepper, seeded and sliced

For the sauce

2 tablespoons dark brown sugar

½ cup fresh lemon juice

¼ cup tomato paste

⅓ cup water

1 teaspoon ground allspice

1 teaspoon salt

1. Preheat the oven to 350°F (180°C). Line a baking sheet with parchment.

2. Brush the eggplant slices with a little olive oil and sprinkle with coarse salt. Roast on the baking sheet until golden, about 20 minutes. Remove from the oven and leave the oven on.

3. Heat half of the remaining oil in a large saucepan over medium heat. Add the onions and sauté until translucent, 4 to 5 minutes. Arrange at the bottom of a baking pan or casserole deep enough to hold the layers (see the photograph). Arrange half of the tomatoes on top of the onions and then layer on all the eggplant.

4. Heat the remaining oil in the same pan the onions were sautéed in and fry the fish fillets briefly, skin-side down, only until golden and crispy, about 1 minute. Arrange the fillets, skin-side up, over the eggplant. Add the rest of the tomatoes on top of the fish and sprinkle the sliced chile over the vegetables.

5. **Prepare the sauce** Mix the brown sugar, lemon juice, tomato paste, water, allspice, and salt in a bowl. Taste, and adjust the seasoning. Pour the sauce over the fish. Cover the baking pan with aluminum foil.

6. Bake for 15 minutes, remove the foil, and bake for another 5 minutes, or until the fish is cooked through. Serve over rice.

VARIATION

ON THE STOVE Arrange the layers in a large wide pan, as explained above. Bring to a boil and simmer, covered, over medium-low heat for 20 minutes. Make sure the contents of the casserole is covered with sauce at all times. Add a little bit of water, if necessary.

INGRIYI | Sweet-and-Sour Beef and Eggplant Casserole

IRAQI

Ruth Oliver: "When I asked my Iraqi relatives for this recipe, I was bombarded with conflicting advice regarding the seasoning, the cooking time, and whatnot. The one thing all cooks agreed upon was that the sauce should be red, slightly tart, and as thick as jam. And how will you know that your ingriyi is a success? When diners wipe their plates clean so they shine."

To achieve that subtle yet distinctive tartness, it is best to use citric acid (available in the vitamin/pharmacy aisles at most supermarkets), but lemon juice is fine too.

Serves 6 to 8

1 pound 10 ounces (about 750 g) stewing beef, such as chuck or brisket, cut into 1-inch (2½-cm) cubes

2 tablespoons tomato paste

¾ cup boiling water

1 teaspoon salt, plus more to taste

¼ teaspoon citric acid or ½ cup lemon juice

3 tablespoons sugar

½ cup vegetable oil

4 medium onions, halved and sliced

8 ripe tomatoes, thinly sliced

4 medium eggplants, peeled and sliced ⅓ inch (1 cm) thick

Freshly ground black pepper

1. Put the meat in a medium pot, add water to cover, season with salt and pepper, and bring to a boil. Skim the foam off the surface, reduce the heat, cover, and simmer for 1 hour until the meat is almost fork tender. Drain and cool slightly.

2. Thoroughly mix together the tomato paste, water, salt, citric acid, and sugar. Taste and adjust the seasoning for a balance of sour, sweet, and salty.

3. Heat the vegetable oil in a large wide pan. Add the onions and sauté until translucent, about 5 minutes. Arrange the cooked meat over the onions and pour over 2 tablespoons of the sauce. Arrange one-third of the tomato slices over the meat in a single layer, then one-third of the eggplant slices. Pour over another 2 tablespoons sauce. Repeat twice more, alternating layers of tomatoes and eggplants and drizzling with the sauce. Season with salt and pepper.

4. Bring to a boil over high heat. Place a plate slightly smaller than the diameter of the pot directly over the eggplants (this will gently press the liquid out of the eggplants and help the sauce reach the desired consistency). Cover the pot and cook over medium-high heat for about 30 minutes. Lower the heat, remove the lid and the plate, and simmer, uncovered, for about 1½ hours, until the contents of the pot are reduced to half the original volume and the sauce is shiny and very thick.

5. Serve over white rice and have plenty of bread to wipe up the sauce.

VARIATION

For an even more flavorful dish, fry the eggplants: Sprinkle them with salt and let stand for 30 minutes to draw out the liquid. Squeeze and pat dry with a kitchen towel. Heat vegetable oil (1 inch/2½ cm deep) in a large wide pan and fry the eggplant slices in one layer (work in batches) on both sides until golden. Transfer to a paper towel–lined plate to absorb the excess oil. Continue as directed in the recipe.

BEEF TONGUE IN A SWEET-AND-SOUR SAUCE

ASHKENAZI

Many people find the notion of cooking or eating tongue off-putting, but I highly recommend getting over it and discovering tongue's velvety texture and delicate flavor. Beef tongue served hot in sweet-and-sour sauce is an Ashkenazi classic, primarily associated with Rosh Hashanah. Tongue is also delicious served cold (without the sauce) with pickles and plenty of mustard or horseradish sauce on the side. The following recipe covers the bases for both options.

Serves 6 to 8

1 beef or veal tongue
(about 2 pounds/1 kg)

1 carrot, sliced into coins

1 bunch celery, diced

2 onions, quartered

6 allspice berries

2 bay leaves

2 garlic cloves, finely chopped

2 tablespoons distilled vinegar or citrus

For the sauce

3 tablespoons vegetable oil

2 onions, diced

3 garlic cloves, minced

2 tablespoons tomato paste

$\frac{1}{2}$ cup raisins

$\frac{1}{2}$ cup dried apricots, halved

$\frac{1}{2}$ cup prunes, pitted and coarsely chopped

2 cups chicken stock or water

2 tablespoons honey

2 tablespoons fresh lemon juice

$\frac{1}{4}$ teaspoon freshly ground black pepper

$\frac{1}{4}$ teaspoon ground allspice

Salt to taste

1. Put the tongue in a large wide pot, cover with water, and bring to a boil. Skim the foam off the surface and add the carrot, celery, onions, allspice, bay leaves, garlic, and vinegar. Return to a boil, reduce the heat, cover, and simmer for about 2½ hours, until tender.

2. Remove the meat from the pan and let cool. Discard the vegetables. Peel the skin from the tongue and trim off any fat and sinew. Boiled tongue can be stored in the refrigerator for up to 2 days in a sealed container.

3. **Prepare the sauce** Heat the vegetable oil in a saucepan over medium heat. Add the onions and sauté until golden.

4. Add the garlic, tomato paste, raisins, apricots, prunes, chicken stock, honey, lemon juice, pepper, allspice, and salt. Bring to a boil and simmer for 10 minutes, until the sauce is thickened. The sauce can be kept refrigerated for up to 2 days.

5. When ready to serve, warm the sauce in a wide pan. Slice the tongue into ⅓-inch (1-cm) slices and add to the pan with the sauce. Cook for about 20 minutes to allow the flavors to meld. Serve with mashed potatoes.

6. **To serve cold** Slice the tongue and serve (without the sauce) with chrain (see page 25), mustard, and pickles.

NORTH AFRICAN FISH STEW, TWO WAYS

There is an ongoing dispute between Moroccan and Tunisian cooks as to who makes a better spicy fish stew. It might put me in a tight spot with both sides, but in my opinion they are not that different. In both cases, fish chunks are nestled in a fiery red sauce. Tunisian chreime is traditionally served on its own, with thick slices of bread to mop up the tasty sauce. The Moroccan version is scented with fresh cilantro, enhanced with peppers (hot and sweet), and usually served over couscous. Because the sauce is so dominant, inexpensive frozen fish fillets can be used in both recipes, but if you're using fresh saltwater fish (snapper, grouper, or halibut), the dish will be even better.

Moroccan Spicy Fish Ragù | MOROCCAN

Serves 4 to 6

½ cup olive oil

10 garlic cloves

2 red bell peppers, quartered, membranes and seeds removed

1 to 2 fresh red chile peppers, halved and seeded

3 dried mild red chile peppers, seeded (optional)

1 cup fresh cilantro, coarsely chopped

1 cup fresh parsley, coarsely chopped

2 tablespoons sweet paprika

Salt to taste

2 cups water

Six 6-ounce (150-g) pieces of grouper, halibut, or other white-fleshed saltwater fish (with the center bone)

1 lemon, cut into wedges

Every time I make this dish, I am amazed at how something so spectacular can be so easy to make. In Israel, fresh grouper, the king of Mediterranean fish, is considered ideal for this recipe. In North America, I have prepared it a few times with fresh halibut, with delicious results.

1. Heat the olive oil in a large wide pan. Add the garlic, bell peppers, and fresh chiles and sauté for 2 minutes. Add the dried chiles (if using), cilantro, parsley, paprika, and salt and sauté for a couple more minutes, stirring occasionally. Pour in the water and bring to a simmer.

2. Cover and cook for 20 minutes. Remove the lid and cook for another 5 to 10 minutes, until the sauce thickens. Taste and adjust the seasoning (once you add the fish, it will be difficult to stir the sauce and play with the flavors).

3. Carefully add the fish chunks (in one layer), cover, and simmer gently for about 15 minutes. Turn the fish and cook for 5 more minutes. Turn off the heat and let stand, covered, for 20 minutes before serving. Serve with lemon wedges over couscous or with thick slices of bread to mop up the sauce.

VARIATIONS

• The dish can also be prepared with boneless fillets. In this case, cook the sauce without the fish. When it is ready (it should be thick, spicy, and flavorful), add the fillets and cook in the sauce for just 8 to 10 minutes.

• To make the fish even more flavorful, marinate it briefly: Combine ⅓ cup olive oil with 2 tablespoons fresh lemon juice and 1 tablespoon paprika. Brush the fish chunks with the mixture and let marinate for 15 minutes. Add to the sauce as directed in the recipe.

Chreime | Tunisian Spicy Fish Ragù

Serves 4 to 6

½ cup olive oil

3 to 4 garlic cloves, minced

1 heaping teaspoon cayenne pepper

2 tablespoons tomato paste

⅓ cup fresh lemon juice

1 tablespoon ground cumin

1½ teaspoons ground caraway

Salt to taste

Six 6-ounce (150-g) pieces of grouper, halibut, or other white-fleshed saltwater fish (with the center bone)

1 lemon, cut into wedges

This is a truly minimalist recipe—chunks of choice fish and a simple sauce, based on the unbeatable combination of cayenne pepper, garlic, cumin, and a dash of ground caraway. Please don't omit any of the spices; they are crucial for the final taste. And be forewarned: Chreime is meant to be really hot. If you are not into spicy, go for another recipe.

1. Heat the olive oil in a large wide pan over medium heat. Add the garlic, cayenne, tomato paste, and lemon juice and bring to a simmer, stirring constantly. Add the cumin, caraway, and salt and stir well.

2. Add the fish pieces in one layer and bring to a simmer. Add water to cover and bring to a boil. Reduce the heat and simmer over low heat for 15 minutes, partially covered. Cover fully and let stand for 20 minutes before serving with lemon wedges and plenty of white bread.

GHORMEH SABZI | Beef and Herb Stew

PERSIAN

Ghormeh in Farsi means "stew," of which there are quite a lot in Persian cuisine. Sabzi means "herbs" and sometimes refers to the fresh herbs that accompany a traditional meal. Diners munch on them between courses to refresh the palate and spike the appetite. Herbs are the basis of this classic beef casserole. Besides loads of chopped herbs, this dish owes its flavor to freshly squeezed lemon juice as well as lemon omani, Persian dried limes. The latter are available at Middle Eastern groceries, some Indian stores, and online (see Mail Order Sources, page 203). The preparation is simple except for chopping large amounts of herbs. It is perfectly fine to pulse them in a food processor as long as you make sure you stop before they become mushy (see the tip on washing and chopping herbs on page 110).

Serves 6 to 8

$\frac{1}{2}$ cup vegetable oil

3 large onions, chopped

2 pounds (1 kg) stewing beef, such as chuck or brisket, cut into $1\frac{1}{2}$-inch (4-cm) cubes

$\frac{3}{4}$ cup kidney beans, soaked overnight and drained

2 Persian dried limes (lemon omani)

Salt to taste

1 teaspoon freshly ground black pepper

1 teaspoon ground turmeric

5 cups boiling water

2 bunches fresh parsley, finely chopped

1 bunch fresh dill, finely chopped

1 bunch fresh cilantro, finely chopped

1 bunch celery leaves, finely chopped

1 bunch scallions (white and green parts), finely chopped

1 leek (light part only), finely chopped

$\frac{1}{3}$ to $\frac{1}{2}$ cup fresh lemon juice

1. Heat $\frac{1}{4}$ cup of the vegetable oil in a large saucepan over medium heat. Add the onions and sauté for 8 to 10 minutes, until soft and golden. Add the meat and brown well on all sides.

2. Add the beans, dried limes, salt, pepper, turmeric, and boiling water and bring to a boil. Cover and cook over low heat for about 1 hour.

3. Heat the remaining $\frac{1}{4}$ cup oil in a separate saucepan. Add the parsley, dill, cilantro, celery, scallions, and leek and sauté for about 7 minutes, until they wilt and become bright green and shiny. Season with salt, transfer to the pan with the meat, and mix gently. Partially cover and gently simmer until the meat is very tender, $1\frac{1}{2}$ hours.

4. Add the lemon juice and cook for another 5 minutes. Taste and adjust the seasoning. Serve over rice.

Meatless Mains

There is no joy without partaking of meat," proclaims the Talmud. And indeed, in Jewish homes, important meals center around meat or fish. Vegetarian dishes are considered mundane, fit for routine weekday meals. But times change, and as many of us prefer to eat less meat or abstain from it entirely, this wholesome meatless fare is rediscovered and cherished, especially in Israel, where vegetables are the mainstay of local cooking. I often find myself serving a vegetarian (or almost vegetarian) Friday-night dinner or Shabbat lunch, and no one complains.

SHAKSHUKA | Eggs Poached in Spicy Tomato Sauce

TUNISIAN, LIBYAN

I spent an improbable amount of time trying to find the definitive recipe for shakshuka, only to realize that there is no such thing. This simple and piquant egg-and-tomato stew is an all-Israeli favorite and has even become famous abroad. There is no ultimate recipe for it because shakshuka is intuitive, forgiving, and versatile. So here is a really nice basic recipe, followed by some tips and variations. Once you start making shakshuka, you will surely develop your own formula. So grab a half dozen free-range eggs, juicy ripe tomatoes, and shukshake it. This one is based on filfel chuma, a Tunisian garlic-and-chile spread that is easy to make and can be stored for months.

Serves 4 to 6

8 to 10 juicy ripe tomatoes, coarsely chopped

3 tablespoons olive oil

5 garlic cloves, minced

1 to 2 fresh chile peppers, seeded and chopped (optional)

2 tablespoons filfel chuma (page 104) or harissa (page 7 or store-bought)

Salt and freshly ground black pepper

6 to 8 eggs (preferably organic or free range)

1. Heat the olive oil in a large deep skillet over medium heat. Add the garlic and chile and stir well. Stir in the filfel chuma and sauté for a minute or so until fragrant, taking care not to burn it.

2. Add the tomatoes, increase the heat, and cook for 3 to 4 minutes, until the tomatoes have released some of their juices. Reduce the heat, cover and simmer for 20 minutes. Season with salt and pepper, taste, and adjust the seasoning. The sauce must be flavorful, spicy, and fully cooked. Once the eggs are added, it is difficult to stir and adjust the seasoning. Up to this point, the sauce can be made ahead and stored in the fridge for 3 to 4 days or frozen for up to a month.

3. When ready to serve, bring the sauce to a boil, then, with a spoon, create 6 to 8 craters in the sauce. Carefully crack the eggs, one by one, into a crater.

4. Cook for 5 to 8 minutes, depending on how you like your eggs cooked (I prefer them slightly runny). Serve at once from the skillet, accompanied by lots of soft white bread or challah.

TIPS AND VARIATIONS

• If tomatoes are not in season, it is better to use high-quality canned ones (for this recipe you will need two 14-ounce/400-g cans).

• Jazz up the sauce with one or more of the following: $\frac{1}{2}$ teaspoon ground caraway, 1 teaspoon ground cumin, $\frac{1}{2}$ teaspoon ground cardamom. Don't add all of them at once; taste as you go.

• To make sure the eggs are cooked evenly, they should be at room temperature.

• For a prettier and more flavorful shakshuka, separate the yolks from the whites and use only the yolks. Reserve the remaining egg whites for another recipe or stir one or two into the sauce (before adding the yolks) to thicken it.

• Covering the skillet once the eggs are added will speed up the process, but it will create a white film over the yolks. *(continued)*

- **SHAKSHUKA WITH ROASTED PEPPERS** Roast 2 to 3 sweet red bell peppers over an open flame or under the broiler until the skin is charred. Let cool in a sealed container or in a closed plastic bag. Peel, remove the seeds, and chop coarsely. Add the bell peppers to the sauce when it is almost ready and cook for 5 minutes before adding the eggs.

- **SHAKSHUKA WITH EGGPLANT** Cut 1 large eggplant into small cubes. Arrange on a baking sheet, drizzle with olive oil, sprinkle with coarse salt, and roast in a 400°F (200°C) oven for 20 minutes, until the eggplant is soft and deep golden. Add to the sauce when it is almost ready and cook for 2 to 3 minutes before adding the eggs.

- **SHAKSHUKA WITH FETA** Crumble ½ cup good-quality feta cheese over the eggs when they are almost done and heat through only until the cheese starts to melt.

Filfel Chuma

Like its close relative harissa (page 7), filfel chuma is prepared from dried sweet and hot peppers and garlic. This version, based on paprika, offers a considerable shortcut, but works only if the spices are of the highest quality.

10 garlic cloves, minced	1 scant teaspoon ground cumin
1 teaspoon high-quality hot paprika	½ cup vegetable oil, plus
4 tablespoons high-quality sweet paprika	2 tablespoons for storing
	2 tablespoons fresh lemon juice
1 scant teaspoon ground caraway	1 teaspoon salt

Mix the garlic, hot paprika, sweet paprika, caraway, cumin, ½ cup of the vegetable oil, the lemon juice, and salt into a smooth paste. Taste and adjust the seasoning. Transfer to a sterilized jar, cover with the remaining 2 tablespoons oil to prevent spoilage, and store in the refrigerator. It keeps for a long time.

TÜRLÜ | Mixed Vegetables Casserole

SEPHARDIC, TURKISH

The ingredients couldn't be simpler: vegetables, tomato paste, water, salt, a dash of sugar. But the result is so much more than the sum of its parts. The secret is precision and attention to details. No wonder that chefs Ella Shine and Orna Agmon—known for their simple and precise approach to cooking—fell in love with this Turkish classic and made it one of the signature dishes at their restaurant Orna and Ella (one of my favorite places in Tel Aviv). The menu lists it as Rice with Vegetables—so typical of Orna and Ella to give this gem such an unassuming name.

Serves 6 to 8

½ cup vegetable oil

2 large onions, cut into 1-inch (2½-cm) cubes

9 ounces (250 g) green beans, trimmed

2 large red bell peppers, seeded and cut into 1½-inch (4-cm) pieces

½ hot green chile pepper, seeded and thinly sliced

5 garlic cloves, thinly sliced

½ butternut squash (about 1 pound/500 g), peeled and cut into 1-inch (2½-cm) cubes

2 medium zucchini, quartered lengthwise and then halved

1 small eggplant, cut into 1½-inch (4-cm) pieces

2 medium potatoes, cut into 1-inch (2½-cm) cubes

2 tomatoes, blanched for 30 seconds, peeled, and diced

1 tablespoon salt, plus more to taste

Freshly ground black pepper

1 tablespoon sugar

1 tablespoon tomato paste

For Garnish

2 tablespoons olive oil

1 cup pumpkin seeds

1. Heat the vegetable oil in a very large sauté pan. Start adding the vegetables in the following order in 4- to 5-minute intervals: onions, beans, bell peppers, chile, garlic, squash, zucchini, and eggplant. Sauté until golden. Add the potatoes and tomatoes. Season with the salt, pepper, and sugar and sauté for another minute. Stir in the tomato paste and cook for 1 minute.

2. Add water so it reaches to one-third of the height of the vegetables. Bring to a boil, reduce the heat, cover, and simmer for 30 minutes.

3. Preheat the oven to 380°F (190°C).

4. Taste the sauce and adjust the seasoning. If it is too tart, add more sugar. With a slotted spoon, remove the vegetables and arrange in a large baking sheet in one layer. Pour over the liquids from the sauté pan. Roast in the oven for 30 minutes, or until the vegetables turn golden brown.

5. **Prepare the garnish** Meanwhile, heat the olive oil in a large sauté pan. Add the pumpkin seeds, season with salt and pepper, and toss over medium heat until the seeds change color to golden green.

6. Mound the vegetables on a serving plate and sprinkle with the toasted pumpkin seeds. In the restaurant, türlü are served over a combination of white and wild rice. They are also delicious over couscous or on their own, as a warm salad.

SPINACH FLAN

ris Gelbart, food editor at *Al Hashulchan* magazine, comes from a line of terrific cooks of Turkish origin. Here is what she told me about this beloved family recipe: "Grandpa Pepo would return from the market with bags of spinach. Grandma Ines would lay it all out on the table and begin to clean the stems. She would then soak the leaves in water to remove all the sand. A lot of work, but watching her many grandchildren fighting over who would get the biggest slice made it all worth it."

Makes one 17 x 12-inch (43 x 30-cm) flan

1 pound (½ kg) spinach, stems removed, leaves rinsed and finely chopped

8 ounces (250 g) feta cheese, crumbled

4 eggs

3 slices day-old white bread, soaked in water, squeezed well, and crumbled

7 tablespoons extra virgin olive oil

4 tablespoons bread crumbs or matzo meal

⅔ cup grated aged sheep's cheese (kashkaval, Greek kasseri, or pecorino)

1. Preheat the oven to 350°F (180°C).

2. Combine the spinach, feta, eggs, crumbled bread, and 5 tablespoons of the olive oil in a large bowl. Mix thoroughly with a wooden spoon or knead with your hands.

3. Grease a 17 x 12-inch (43 x 30-cm) baking pan with 1 tablespoon of the olive oil and dust with a thin layer of bread crumbs (about 2 tablespoons).

4. Pour the mixture into the pan. Drizzle with the remaining 1 tablespoon olive oil. Sprinkle with the remaining bread crumbs and cover with the grated cheese.

5. Bake for 30 minutes, or until set and golden. Slice into squares and serve warm.

FETA-STUFFED PEPPER "CUTLETS"

BULGARIAN

Roasted peppers and feta cheese—this combo epitomizes Bulgarian cuisine. The following recipe, nicknamed "fake schnitzel" in Israel, yields a delightful snack: golden and crispy on the outside; red, oozing cheese and juicy on the inside. Serve as a starter or a vegetarian main dish. For a vegan version, you can leave out the cheese.

Serves 4 to 5

4 to 5 large red bell peppers

11 ounces (300 g) feta cheese, cut into eight to ten 1-inch (2½-cm)-thick slices

⅓ cup unbleached all-purpose flour

Salt and freshly ground black pepper

1 egg, beaten

½ cup good-quality unseasoned bread crumbs (preferably panko or homemade)

2 thyme sprigs, leaves only

Vegetable oil for frying

1. Preheat the oven to 400°F (200°C) and line a baking sheet with parchment.

2. Arrange the bell peppers on the baking sheet and roast, turning once or twice, until the skins are charred. Transfer to a plastic container and close. Allow to cool (the peppers' skins will separate from the flesh). Peel and remove the seeds and membranes. Try to keep the peppers whole, but if they tear, don't worry—the breading will glue everything back together.

3. Stuff each pepper with 2 slices of the cheese.

4. Prepare three plates: one with the flour seasoned with salt and pepper, one with the beaten egg diluted with a little water, and one with the bread crumbs seasoned with thyme. Dip the stuffed peppers in the flour and gently shake off the excess. Dip the peppers in the beaten egg and, finally, dip in the bread crumbs and press together firmly to ensure good adhesion and to form a nice coating. To prevent the stuffing from seeping out, dip the whole pepper once again in the egg and bread crumbs.

5. Heat the vegetable oil in a heavy frying pan until it simmers. The oil level should be one-half the thickness of the cutlets. Add the cutlets and fry over medium heat for 2 minutes on each side, until golden. Remove from the oil to a paper towel–lined plate to absorb the excess oil. Serve promptly.

SABZI POLO | Rice Pilaf with Lots and Lots of Fresh Herbs

PERSIAN

The first time I prepared this dish I was sure that the ratio of 3 cups of herbs to 3 cups of rice was outrageous, so I reduced it to a sensible 1 cup of herbs. The result was pleasant but predictable. The next time I stuck to the original recipe and the difference was apparent—a brilliantly green rice pilaf that smelled like a springtime meadow. As for the combination of herbs, feel free to skip one or another that you don't have or don't like. Do not, however, omit the dill, which is crucial to the flavor. In Persian cuisine this pilaf is traditionally served with fried fish. But it is also great on its own.

Serves 8

3 cups basmati rice

3 tablespoons vegetable oil

1 large onion, finely chopped

1 teaspoon salt

½ teaspoon ground cumin

¼ teaspoon ground turmeric

½ teaspoon freshly ground black pepper

3 cardamom pods, crushed, or dash of ground cardamom

3 cups (about 5 bunches) combination of fresh parsley, dill, and cilantro, finely chopped by hand or pulsed in a food processor

4½ cups boiling water

2 tablespoons unsalted butter (optional)

1. Wash the rice several times under running water until the water runs clear. Soak the rice for 20 minutes in cold water. Rinse, drain, and set aside.

2. Heat the vegetable oil in a large heavy saucepan over medium heat. Add the onion and sauté until golden, 7 to 8 minutes. Add the salt, cumin, turmeric, pepper, cardamom, herbs, and boiling water and cook for 5 minutes. Taste and adjust the seasoning. The broth should be flavorful and quite salty.

3. Add the rice and cook uncovered over medium heat, until the liquid is just absorbed, about 5 minutes. Stir gently to distribute the herbs throughout the rice.

4. Cover with a tight-fitting lid and cook over very low heat for 10 minutes. Remove from the heat, fluff the rice, cover again, and let rest for 15 minutes. Stir in the butter (if using) and serve.

TIP

Many recipes in this book call for chopping large amounts of herbs. To streamline the process, I wash my herbs after chopping and have found the following method to be the most convenient: Leave the bunch tied and chop off the stalks (as most recipes call for leaves only; stalks can be reserved for flavoring soups and stews). Keeping the bunch together, chop the leaves, transfer them to a fine sieve, and wash thoroughly under running water. Let dry in a sieve for 15 minutes or more. If the herbs are used for cooking, it doesn't matter if they are a bit damp.

COUSCOUS WITH VEGETABLES (OR TUESDAY COUSCOUS)

NORTH AFRICAN

Tuesday is the couscous day in Jewish North African families. I have heard many explanations for this custom, most having to do with the fact that Tuesday was the weekly laundry day. I am a bit vague as to how these two tasks are connected, and in any case in the washing-machine age it is no longer relevant. Curiously, this tradition has not only survived in modern-day Israel but has even spread beyond the North African community. Everywhere—in army canteens, workplace dining halls, and even restaurants—couscous is served on Tuesdays, and it is usually vegetarian. Of course, it is also served for Friday-night dinners and on holidays, with more elaborate trimmings. Serve it with two traditional sides—Chershi (page 33) and Messayir (page 32)—and you will have an authentic Tuesday couscous meal.

Serves 6 to 8

For the vegetables

¾ cup dried chickpeas, soaked overnight in water

3 carrots, cut into large chunks

3 potatoes, peeled and quartered

2 onions, quartered

1 tablespoon extra virgin olive oil

2 large zucchini, cut into large chunks

1 pound (½ kg) butternut squash or pumpkin, cut into large chunks

1 small green cabbage, core removed, quartered

3 celery stalks with the leaves, halved crosswise

1 teaspoon salt

½ teaspoon freshly ground black pepper

½ teaspoon ground turmeric

For the couscous

1 pound (½ kg) instant couscous

2½ cups boiling water

1 teaspoon salt

½ teaspoon freshly ground black pepper

10 saffron threads, diluted in ¼ cup boiling water until the water turns orange (optional)

3 tablespoons extra virgin olive oil

I. Prepare the vegetables Drain the soaked chickpeas and put them in a large pot. Add 6 cups water, cover, and cook over medium-low heat for 45 minutes, or until the chickpeas are almost tender. Add the carrots, potatoes, onions, and olive oil and cook for 20 minutes.

2. Add the zucchini, squash, cabbage, and celery. Season with the salt, pepper, and turmeric and cook for 15 minutes, or until the zucchini and squash are fork tender. Taste and adjust the seasoning. The vegetables can be cooked in advance and heated before serving.

3. Prepare the couscous Mix the instant couscous with the boiling water in a large bowl (if you are using the saffron, reduce the water to 2¼ cups) and season with the salt, pepper, and diluted saffron (if using). Let stand for 10 minutes until the grains swell. Add the olive oil and rub the couscous between your palms or fluff it with a fork (to obtain finer crumbs and airier texture).

4. Steam in a double boiler or heat, covered, in a microwave for 5 minutes.

5. To serve, mound the couscous in a deep dish. Using a slotted serving spoon, arrange the vegetables around or on top of the couscous. Ladle the liquid (about ½ cup per serving) around the couscous: The idea is just to add moisture to the grains, not soak them with too much liquid. Serve at once.

Making the Best of Instant Couscous

Real couscous (made from scratch from semolina mixed with water, rubbed between palms, passed repeatedly through a sieve to form fine crumbs, and then mixed with oil and cooked in a double boiler called a couscoussier) has inimitable texture, but making it is labor intensive and requires skill. Thankfully, instant couscous is a very good substitute and busy cooks all over the world have adopted it in their kitchens. Lately, I have discovered whole-grain instant couscous, which in my opinion has superior taste, in addition to being more nutritious.

TAHDIG | Rice Pilaf with Dried Apricots and Crispy Potato Crust

PERSIAN

Persian cuisine has a number of magnificent rice dishes in its repertoire. Here's one of the standouts. The rice is rinsed thoroughly and cooked twice—first boiled rapidly in a large amount of water, like pasta, then steamed over low heat nestled over tahdig, a layer of potatoes at the bottom of a pot. The tahdig turns golden brown and crunchy while the rice is cooking and prevents it from drying up. Before serving, the casserole is turned upside down onto a large platter so that the tahdig ends up on the top. Usually tahdig is fried in oil, but in this recipe (suitable for vegetarian and dairy meals), it is fried in butter with egg and yogurt, which makes it even more delicious. To make sure the tahdig doesn't stick to the bottom, it is best to use a nonstick pan.

Serves 6 to 8

2½ cups long-grain rice

3¼ teaspoons salt

1 cup chopped fresh herbs, such as parsley, dill, tarragon, chives, and cilantro

1 cup dried apricots

2 tablespoons plain yogurt (not low fat)

1 egg

4 tablespoons unsalted butter

2 Yukon Gold or yellow potatoes, peeled and sliced ⅓ inch (1 cm) thick

1. Rinse the rice several times under running water until the water runs clear. Drain, place in a bowl, and stir in 2 teaspoons of the salt. Add water so it comes 2 inches (5 cm) above the level of the rice and let sit for 30 minutes. Drain the rice.

2. Fill a medium pot with water so it is three-quarters full. Add 1 teaspoon of the salt and bring to a boil. Add the rice, stir gently, and bring to a boil again. Cook, uncovered, over medium heat for about 3 minutes, until the rice is al dente (the inside of the grain is still firm).

3. Transfer the rice to a colander and rinse with cold water. Mix in the herbs and apricots.

4. Beat the yogurt with the egg in a small bowl.

5. Melt the butter in a medium saucepan (preferably nonstick) over medium heat and add 1 tablespoon water. Arrange the potato slices to cover the bottom of the pan in one layer and pour the yogurt-egg mixture over them.

6. Sprinkle a thin layer of rice over the top and flatten gently (this, together with the potatoes, will form the tahdig). Mix the rice with the remaining ¼ teaspoon salt and arrange over the tahdig. Gently spoon in about ⅓ cup water. Using the handle of a wooden spoon, poke through the rice to create 4 to 5 "chimneys" all the way down until it hits a potato (this will ensure that the rice cooks evenly). Cover the pot with a towel (a paper towel is fine, too) and a tight-fitting lid. Cook for 2 to 3 minutes over medium heat, reduce the heat to the minimum, and cook for 40 minutes.

7. Remove the lid and flip the pot upside down onto a large platter, so that the tahdig is on top.

VARIATION

FOR A VEGAN (NONDAIRY) VERSION Fry the potato slices in 2 to 3 tablespoons vegetable oil until they become golden. Flip them and fry on the other side. Flatten some of the rice over this and continue as directed.

MUJADDARA | Rice with Lentils

SYRIAN, EGYPTIAN

This classic Middle Eastern specialty is popular with Jewish communities in Syria, Egypt, and Iraq. In Israel, it has become a ubiquitous rice side dish. It is also a nutritious main course for vegetarians (it contains both grains and legumes), especially if you make it with brown rice. I like serving it with a bowl of thick yogurt or tahini spread (see page 159) as an accompaniment or garnished with thick yogurt.

Serves 6 to 8

2 cups basmati or long-grain rice

1½ cups brown or black lentils

2 tablespoons olive oil

3 large onions, chopped

1 teaspoon ground cumin

1 teaspoon ground cinnamon

½ teaspoon turmeric (optional)

Salt and freshly ground black pepper

For the Garnish

2 to 3 tablespoons olive oil

2 large onions, thinly sliced into rings

1. Wash the rice several times under running water until the water runs clear. Soak the rice for 20 minutes in cold water. Rinse, drain, and set aside.

2. Cook the lentils in 4 cups water until they soften, about 20 minutes. Drain, reserving 1 cup of the cooking liquid, and set aside.

3. Heat the 1 tablespoon olive oil in a saucepan (suitable for cooking the rice) over medium heat. Add the chopped onions and sauté until golden, 6 to 7 minutes. Add the lentils and season with the cumin, cinnamon, turmeric (if using), salt, and pepper. Add the rice and stir-fry for a minute or two until the rice grains turn opaque.

4. Add 2 cups boiling water and the reserved cooking liquid. Bring to a boil, lower the heat, cover with a tight-fitting lid, and simmer for 20 minutes. Turn off the heat, fluff with a fork, cover, and let rest for 10 minutes.

5. Before serving, prepare the garnish Heat the 2 to 3 tablespoons olive oil in a skillet. Add the onion rings and fry on medium heat for 10 minutes, or until brown and crisp. Arrange over the mujaddara and serve at once.

VARIATIONS

BROWN RICE MUJADDARA Soak 2 cups brown basmati rice in cold water for at least 2 hours (or up to 12 hours—the longer the rice is soaked, the faster it will cook). Proceed as directed, but cook the dish in 3 cups water plus the 1 cup reserved cooking liquid. Cook for about 30 minutes, until the rice is tender.

RICE, LENTIL, AND EGGPLANT SALAD I stumbled upon this recipe by accident, when I had some leftover mujaddara in the fridge, and it has become one of our family favorites: To 3 cups of cold prepared mujaddara, add 1 roasted eggplant (cube, sprinkle with coarse salt and olive oil, and roast for 20 to 30 minutes in a hot oven until deep golden). Toss with ⅓ cup chopped fresh cilantro and some fresh lemon juice. Taste and adjust the seasoning. Serve at room temperature with a bowl of yogurt seasoned with cumin, minced garlic, salt, pepper, and chopped fresh mint.

"BEFORE SHABBAT" PASTA CASSEROLE

BULGARIAN

In many Jewish households, Friday lunch is light and often vegetarian, so as not to inconvenience the cook who is too busy with Shabbat preparations—and to leave room for the big Friday-night dinner. In Jewish Bulgarian homes, this crusty casserole is served. It's also a great way to make use of pasta and cheese leftovers.

Serves 4 to 6

2½ cups cooked pasta (preferably spaghetti) or, if you're cooking it from scratch, 12 ounces (350 g) dried

4 ounces (100 g) feta cheese, crumbled

9 ounces (250 g) cottage cheese

3 eggs

Salt and freshly ground black pepper

¼ teaspoon freshly grated nutmeg (optional)

½ stick (2 ounces/50 g) unsalted butter, cut into small cubes

1. Preheat the oven to 350°F (180°C).

2. Combine the pasta, feta, cottage cheese, and eggs in a large bowl. Taste and season with the salt, pepper, and nutmeg (if using).

3. Transfer the mixture to a baking dish of your choice (a thinner casserole will be crispier, a thicker one, juicier). Sprinkle with the butter and bake for 40 minutes, or until the top is golden brown. Serve at once.

VARIATION

For a richer, gratinlike casserole, add ½ cup heavy cream and/or ⅓ cup grated hard cheese, such as kashkaval (see page 140), pecorino, Parmesan, or Cheddar.

GREEN MASALA BEANS

INDIAN (BENE ISRAEL)

Nurit Brown is a descendant of Bene Israel, the historic Jewish community of India. The Bene Israel ("Sons of Israel") are believed to have been one of the Lost Tribes. Or, according to a different theory (of which, as a foodie, I am fond), they are descendants of olive oil producers from the Galilee who settled in western India. After India gained its independence in 1947 and Israel was established in 1948, many Bene Israel immigrated to Israel. Nurit's family left India when she was a little girl, but she still cooks the family's recipes. Her secret ingredient is a paste of green chiles, garlic, and cilantro that she calls green masala, and it is quite similar to Yemenite zhug (see page 162). Nurit makes a batch and keeps it in the refrigerator to be used over the week in different recipes. Here she matches it with fresh green beans.

Serves 6 to 8

2 tablespoons vegetable oil

1 large onion, diced

1 teaspoon salt

½ teaspoon ground turmeric

1 tablespoon green masala (see below)

1 pound (½ kg) green beans, stem ends trimmed, cut crosswise into ½-inch (¼-cm) pieces

½ cup water

I. Heat the vegetable oil in a large pot. Add the onion and sauté until golden. Add the salt, turmeric, green masala, and green beans. Mix well and add the water.

2. Cover and cook over medium-low heat for about 30 minutes, until the beans are somewhat translucent. Stir occasionally to prevent burning. Add more water by the tablespoon, if needed. The dish is not supposed to make gravy, so add just enough water to prevent the beans from sticking to the pot.

3. Serve with basmati rice and a mango pickle (available at Indian groceries and the ethnic food aisles of the supermarket).

Green Masala

You can double and triple the amount and freeze the masala in small Ziploc bags. When frozen, add to simmering pots and allow for some extra time for the paste to thaw and release its aromas.

½ pound fresh cilantro

¼ pound hot chile peppers, such as jalapeño or any other chile, depending on how hot you like your food

5 garlic cloves

1 teaspoon salt

Grind the cilantro, chiles, and garlic together in a meat grinder or pulse in a food processor. Add the salt. Refrigerate for up to 1 week for use in many recipes. It can also be frozen.

Savory Pastries

Throughout this book I have tried to pick relatively user-friendly recipes and streamline their preparation. In this chapter, however, there is no way to evade kneading, rolling, shaping, and filling. With a few exceptions (Sfikha, page 137, or Bouikous, page 135), these special-occasion treats take some time to prepare and require basic baking skills. Oh, but the smell that drives everybody crazy while they bake, the oohs and aahs of the guests—aren't these worth a little effort?

KA'AK | Savory Sesame Cookies

SEPHARDIC

Grandmothers usually have them in the kitchen cabinet—well hidden in a tin box, waiting for the occasional guest. Also referred to as biscochos in Ladino, these loop-shaped cookies are quite hard (perfect for dipping in hot mint tea) and have a mildly savory flavor. Usually they are coated with sesame and often seasoned with mahlab, a fragrant spice made from cherry seeds. Micky Shemo, a well-known Israeli pastry chef, has transformed this homey snack into something pretty luxurious—he adds small amounts of yeast and baking powder to make the pastry pleasantly flaky and incorporates sesame seeds into the dough for extra richness. He also replaces mahlab with caraway seeds that are more accessible and add aroma and crunch.

Makes about 50 cookies

3 cups (14½ ounces/420 g) unbleached all-purpose flour

10 tablespoons (1¼ sticks; 5 ounces/150 g) unsalted butter

1 teaspoon baking powder

⅓ teaspoon instant yeast

½ cup (2½ ounces/70 g) sesame seeds, plus 1 cup sesame seeds (or a combination of regular and black sesame seeds) for coating

2¾ fluid ounces (80 ml/⅓ cup) water

2¾ fluid ounces (80 ml/⅓ cup) vegetable oil

1 tablespoon salt

1 tablespoon caraway seeds

2 eggs, beaten

1. Combine the flour, butter, baking powder, yeast, the ½ cup sesame seeds, water, vegetable oil, salt, and caraway seeds in the bowl of a stand mixer fitted with a dough hook and knead for 3 to 4 minutes to a smooth dough.

2. Cover the bowl with a kitchen towel and let stand at room temperature for 1 hour. The dough will not rise considerably but will be much easier to handle.

3. Punch down the dough and divide it into 3 equal parts. Roll each part into a log 1 inch (2½ cm) in diameter. Slice each log into ⅓-inch (1-cm) disks and roll each disk into a thin rope about 5 inches (12 cm) long. Connect the ends to shape small loops.

4. Preheat the oven to 340°F (170°C). Line two baking sheets with parchment.

5. Pour the beaten eggs into a small bowl and put the 1 cup sesame seeds in another. Dip the top part of each cookie in the beaten egg and then in the sesame seeds. Arrange on the baking sheets.

6. Bake for 30 to 35 minutes, until golden. Cool completely and store in an airtight tin at room temperature for up to 10 days.

ADJARULI KHACHAPURI | Cheese and Egg–Filled Pies

GEORGIAN

When I was ten, still living in the Soviet Union, I went with my family for a vacation in Abkhazia, a province of Georgia. The memories that I retain from that trip are all sensory: the sharp, cool scent of cilantro that grew everywhere, the musky aroma of ripe figs, and the taste of a crusty cheesy pie our Jewish landlady baked for us. Many years later, when I bit into a khachapuri in a Georgian bakery at Mahane Yehuda Market in Jerusalem, memories from that long-forgotten holiday came rushing back to me.

Georgian cuisine arrived in Israel during the 1970s with a large wave of immigration from the Soviet Union, but for a long time this unique cuisine, merging influences from neighboring Russia, Turkey, and Armenia, remained a secret known only to the somewhat secluded Georgian community. It took two decades and some good Georgian restaurants and bakeries for the Israelis to discover it, and one of the first foods that got noticed was boat-shape khachapuri pies. The original recipe calls for sulguni, a Georgian cheese with a texture similar to mozzarella but with a salty-sour flavor. Here it is replaced by a combination of aged mozzarella and good feta.

Makes 6 pies

For the dough

3½ cups (1 pound 2 ounces/
500 g) unbleached all-purpose or
bread flour, plus more for dusting

⅓ ounce instant yeast

Pinch of salt

10½ ounces (1¼ cups/300 ml) water

1¾ sticks (7 ounces/200 g) unsalted
butter, softened

For the filling

½ cup (4½ ounces/125 g) cottage
cheese

1 egg

9 ounces (250 g) aged mozzarella,
grated

4 ounces (110 g) good-quality feta
cheese, crumbled

For the topping (optional)

6 eggs (1 per pastry)

2 tablespoons unsalted butter, cut
into small cubes

1. Prepare the dough Combine the flour, yeast, salt, water, and butter in the bowl of a stand mixer fitted with a dough hook and knead for about 10 minutes to a soft and slightly sticky dough.

2. Lightly flour the dough in the bowl, cover with plastic wrap, and let rise for about 30 minutes, until doubled in volume.

3. Punch the dough down and divide it into 6 equal-size balls. Cover with a kitchen towel and let rise for another 15 minutes.

4. Preheat the oven to 400°F (200°C). Line two baking sheets with parchment.

5. Prepare the filling Combine the cottage cheese, egg, mozzarella, and feta in a bowl.

6. Work with one piece of dough at a time. With a rolling pin, stretch and flatten the dough into an oval sheet ⅓ inch (1 cm) thick. Place one-sixth of the filling in the center of the oval. Spread to within 1 inch of the edges. Roll the edges over to make a thick rim, pinching the narrow sides of the oval together to form a point at the ends. The pie should look like a kayak (see the photograph). Fill and shape the rest of the pies in the same manner.

7. Slide the pies onto the baking sheets and place on the bottom rack of the oven. Bake for 12 to 15 minutes, until the crust is golden and the bottom is firm and crusty. Remove the pies from the oven, leaving the oven on.

8. Prepare the topping Break the eggs, one at a time, into a small bowl and carefully slide each into the pie. When all the pies are filled with the eggs, return the pan to the oven and bake for 5 minutes. Top each pie with a small cube of butter and serve immediately.

SAMBOUSEK | Chickpea-Filled Pastry Pockets

IRAQI

Those familiar with Indian cuisine will find these flaky chickpea-filled dough pockets similar to Indian samosas. No surprise here—the Jewish Iraqi community had long-standing ties with Indian Jews, which explains many similarities between their cuisines (see page 158 about the Iraqi amba). This delicacy came to my kitchen via Nir Dudek, a psychologist and gifted food writer, complete with a charming story:

> My wife Nirit's grandmama hails from Iraq. Grandma has a friend, Marcel, who is considered one of the best cooks in her neighborhood. Every Friday she would send Nirit's family exactly twenty sambousek, but her hard labor was not rewarded. One person would say, "So-and-so ate too many," while another would complain that he didn't even have a smidge, and Shabbat would be ruined by fights and quibbles. Eventually, Marcel found a solution: She would give every member of the family a personal sambousek bag. Each person would pace himself, eat sambousek at his leisure, and Shabbat peace would be saved.

Makes 40 pastries

For the dough

3½ cups (1 pound 2 ounces/500 g) unbleached all-purpose flour

7 teaspoons (3½ ounces/100 g) cold unsalted butter, cut into small pieces

1 egg

½ teaspoon salt

2¼ teaspoons instant yeast

1 cup (8½ ounces/240 ml) water

For the filling

1 pound (450 g) cooked chickpeas (or frozen or canned, drained and rinsed)

¼ cup vegetable oil

4 medium onions, halved and thinly sliced

½ teaspoon ground cumin

1 to 2 teaspoons salt

½ teaspoon freshly ground black pepper

Vegetable oil for deep-frying

1. Prepare the dough Put the flour and butter in a large bowl and work them with the tips of your fingers until the mixture resembles coarse crumbs. Mix in the egg, salt, yeast, and water. Transfer to a lightly floured work surface and knead for 2 to 3 minutes, until the dough becomes smooth and begins to develop stringy strands of gluten. (Cut a walnut-size piece of the dough and stretch it with your fingers. You should see stretched strings that resemble melted cheese.) Place the dough in a clean bowl, cover with plastic wrap, and let rise for about 1 hour.

2. Meanwhile, prepare the filling Puree the chickpeas in a food processor.

3. Heat the ¼ cup vegetable oil in a large frying pan over medium heat. Add the onions and sauté until golden brown, 7 to 8 minutes. Add the chickpea puree and season with the cumin, salt, and pepper. Cook over medium-low heat, stirring constantly, for 4 to 5 minutes, until golden. Set aside to cool.

4. Line two baking sheets with parchment.

5. Form dough balls the size of golf balls and cover with a towel to prevent them from drying out. Roll out each ball by hand or with a rolling pin into a thin, pliable circle. Put a spoonful of filling in the center, fold the circle in half, and press the dough down into half-moons. Pinch the edges with your fingers or a fork. Arrange in a single layer on the prepared baking sheets. At this point, you can freeze the pastries. (Thaw them 30 minutes before frying.)

6. Heat the vegetable oil for frying in a wide pan over medium heat. Fry the sambousek in batches until golden on both sides. Transfer them to a large colander to drain some of the excess oil and then put on a plate lined with a paper towel.

(continued)

7. Serve on the same day or freeze. When ready to serve, heat for 4 to 5 minutes in a preheated 400°F (200°C) oven.

VARIATIONS

• Add ½ finely chopped green chile pepper to the filling along with the spices.

• **BAKED SAMBOUSEK** Preheat the oven to 350°F (180°C) and line a baking sheet with parchment. Arrange the pies on the parchment and brush with beaten egg. Bake for 25 to 30 minutes, until golden.

• **POTATO AND ONION-FILLED SAMBOUSEK (ALMOST KNISH)** Cook 4 potatoes in their jackets until fork tender. Cool slightly. Meanwhile, slowly sauté 2 chopped onions in ¼ cup vegetable oil until deep golden, about 7 minutes. Peel the potatoes, mash, and mix with the onions (including the oil in which they fried). Season with salt and freshly ground black pepper and a little bit of sweet paprika (optional). Fill and shape as directed in the recipe, then deep-fry or bake.

KÁPOSZTÁS POGÁCSA | Caramelized Cabbage Buns

HUNGARIAN

Cabbage is a magical vegetable that completely changes its personality when cooked—from fresh, bitey, and crunchy to sweet and mellow. Hungarian cooks are intimately familiar with this wonder and take full advantage of it. Take, for example, these truly unique buns. The cabbage is caramelized with some butter and sugar and then added to the dough along with savory cheese. A delicious pastry for a weekend brunch or a Shavuot celebration.

Makes 24 buns

For the cabbage

1 pound (½ kg) green cabbage, very finely chopped

1 tablespoon salt

½ stick (2 ounces/50 grams) unsalted butter

1 tablespoon vegetable oil

1 tablespoon sugar

½ teaspoon white pepper

½ teaspoon sweet Hungarian paprika

For the dough

5⅓ cups (1 pound 10 ounces/750 g) unbleached all-purpose flour

1 ounce (30 g) Parmesan cheese, finely grated

1 tablespoon instant yeast

⅓ cup plus 1 tablespoon (3½ fluid ounces/100 ml) milk

7 ounces (200 ml) sour cream

2 egg yolks

1 tablespoon whole caraway seeds

Salt

½ teaspoon white pepper

2¼ sticks (9 ounces/250 g) unsalted butter, softened

For the glaze

1 egg yolk, beaten

I. Prepare the cabbage Thoroughly rub the chopped cabbage with the salt and set aside for 1 hour to allow the cabbage to soften and release its liquid. Drain well.

2. Heat the butter and vegetable oil in a large pan over medium heat. Add the sugar and stir until golden. Add the cabbage, white pepper, and paprika and lower the heat. Simmer over very low heat for about 30 minutes, stirring occasionally, until the cabbage is golden. Set aside to cool.

3. Prepare the dough Combine the flour, Parmesan, and yeast in the bowl of a stand mixer fitted with the dough hook. Gradually add the milk, sour cream, egg yolks, caraway seeds, salt, and white pepper and continue to knead for about 5 minutes. Add the butter and knead for about 5 minutes, until the dough is pliable and smooth. Add the cabbage and knead for 2 to 3 minutes.

4. Transfer the dough to an oiled bowl, cover, and let rise for 2 hours at room temperature.

5. Roll out the dough on a floured work surface to a thickness of 1 inch (2½ cm). Cut with a cookie cutter, biscuit cutter, or a glass into disks 3 inches (7 cm) in diameter and arrange on two parchment-lined baking sheets. Brush with the egg yolk and, using a fork or toothpick, make a crisscross pattern on the glaze.

6. Allow to rise, uncovered, for 30 minutes. In the meantime, preheat the oven to 400°F (200°C).

7. Bake for about 25 minutes, until golden. Serve the same day or freeze and heat for 4 to 5 minutes in a preheated 400°F (200°C) oven.

LAKHOUKH | Panfried Flat Bread

YEMENI

Early in the morning, at Tel Aviv's HaTikvah market, you will find one of the very last lakhoukh makers in town. Watching him at work is a fascinating spectacle: He's juggling a dozen skillets, cooking up a storm of batter that's turning in a matter of minutes into spongy, crumpetlike flat breads. Customers are gathering around. Some are buying a fresh lakhoukh to take home; others are eating it on the spot. Some are rolling an entire Israeli breakfast into the lakhoukh: an omelet, chopped salad, cheese, and hummus; others are eating it plain, dipped in hilbeh, a Yemenite fenugreek relish.

Lakhoukh is easy to re-create at home, but you will need to cool down the pan between batches (to make sure the lakhoukh's surface is smooth). You can dip the pan's bottom in ice water, run it under cold water, or simply work with two pans—letting one cool down while the other is doing the work. You can use lakhoukh to make wraps and serve it with hot soups. I like it best with butter and honey.

Makes 20 flat breads

3½ cups (1 pound 2 ounces/500 g) unbleached all-purpose flour

1½ teaspoons instant yeast

1 teaspoon baking powder

1 tablespoon salt

1½ teaspoons sugar

3 cups water

Vegetable oil for frying

To serve

Zhug (see page 162)

Grated Tomatoes (see page 162)

1. Combine the flour, yeast, baking powder, salt, sugar, and water in a bowl with a wooden spoon or in a stand mixer fitted with a paddle attachment. Cover with plastic wrap or a towel and let stand for 2 hours (or even for up to 8 hours in the fridge), until the batter doubles in volume.

2. Heat a medium nonstick frying pan and cover with a very thin film of vegetable oil. Wipe the excess oil with a paper towel (no additional oil will be needed during frying). Using a ladle or a pitcher, pour in just enough batter to cover the bottom of the pan and cook over medium heat for 2 to 3 minutes, until bubbles cover the top of the flat bread and the bottom is golden brown—just like pancakes before you flip them, but don't flip!

3. Remove the flat bread from the pan with a spatula and cover with a towel to prevent drying. Cool the pan (see explanation above) and continue with the next batch, until all the batter has been used.

FROJALDA | Cheese Bread

TURKISH

With a texture resembling a rich, savory focaccia bursting with melted cheese, frojalda is the official Shavuot bread in Jewish Turkish families. Serve it warm, fresh from the oven, with vegetable crudités, olives, and pickles. Frojalda is also delicious for sandwiches, especially with smoked or salted fish and cream cheese or tapenade.

Makes one 17 x 12-inch (40 x 30-cm) bread

3½ cups (1 pound 2 ounces/500 g) unbleached all-purpose flour

1½ teaspoons instant yeast

2 cups (17 ounces/480 ml) water

10 ounces (300 g) feta cheese, crumbled

1¾ sticks (7 ounces/200 g) unsalted butter, melted

4 ounces (120 g) young Cheddar or Jack cheese, grated

1. Combine the flour, yeast, and water in a large bowl and knead with your hands until a very soft, almost runny dough is formed. Add the feta and mix until it is fully incorporated into the dough.

2. Pour half of the melted butter into a deep 17 x 12-inch (40 x 30-cm) baking pan. Transfer the dough to the pan, flatten, and pour in the rest of the butter, making sure the dough is covered with butter on all sides.

3. Cover with another deep baking pan, facing down (so that the dough has room to rise), and then cover with a towel and let rise until doubled in volume, 2 to 3 hours.

4. Preheat the oven to 400°F (200°C).

5. Sprinkle the grated cheese over the dough. Bake for 30 to 40 minutes, until golden and crispy.

6. Cut into large squares and serve warm. Frojalda can be stored in the refrigerator for a day or two. Before serving, heat for 10 to 15 minutes in a preheated 400°F (200°C) oven so that the pastry is crispy again.

Shavuot, Balkan Style

The Jews of the Balkans have brought to Israel numerous versions of savory, flaky pies. The pies are usually made with phyllo or puff pastry and almost always incorporate piquant cheese. Here I would like to introduce you to some of the standouts: Banitza (page 140), Bourekas (page 143), Bouikos (page 135), Chukor (page 139), and Frojalda (above). Together they make the most charming Shavuot spread (hands down, the best place to celebrate Shavuot is at the table of a Balkan family). You can also include Spinach Flan (page 106) and Sutlach—sweet rice pudding (page 192).

BOUIKOS CON KASHKAVAL | Mini Cheese Buns

SEPHARDIC

One of the easiest dishes in this chapter, these bite-size snacks are perfect for entertaining. Treat the cheeses listed as guidelines, and feel free to use whatever leftover cheese you have at hand—just make sure you maintain the ratio between hard and soft cheeses. The dough may be prepared in advance, wrapped, and kept in the refrigerator, but the buns must be baked shortly before serving.

Makes 30 bite-size snacks

2½ cups (12½ ounces/350 g) self-rising flour

9 ounces (250 g) ricotta or farmer cheese

7 ounces (200 g) semihard or hard cheese, such as Gruyère, kashkaval, Greek kasseri, or Parmesan, grated

5 ounces (150 g) feta cheese, crumbled

1 egg

1¾ sticks (7 ounces/200 g) unsalted butter, melted

2 ounces (50 g) Gruyère or Parmesan cheese, grated, for coating

1. Preheat the oven to 400°F (200°C). Line a baking sheet with parchment.

2. Combine the flour, ricotta, grated cheese, feta, egg, and butter in a bowl, and mix into a very soft dough. Add some flour if it's too wet.

3. Divide the dough into 30 balls the size of a walnut. Place the coating cheese in a shallow bowl or plate. Dip the dome of each ball into the cheese and arrange the balls, spaced evenly, on the baking sheet.

4. Bake for about 20 minutes, until the buns are golden. Cool slightly and serve at once.

VARIATIONS

• **MULTICOLORED BOUIKOS** Divide the dough into 3 equal parts. To the first part, add 2 tablespoons pesto. To the second part, add 2 tablespoons sun-dried tomato paste. To the third part, add 1 teaspoon ground turmeric (or just leave it plain). Mix each part thoroughly and shape as directed in the recipe.

• **OLIVE-STUFFED BOUIKOS** After shaping the buns, insert 1 large green pitted olive into each one and smooth over. Arrange on the sheet and bake as directed.

• Instead of coating bouikos with grated cheese, use black or white sesame seeds or whole poppy seeds.

SFIKHA | Open-Face Meat Bourekas

SYRIAN

F or me, nothing says Shabbat morning like sfikha," says Roi Antebi, chef-owner of Bertie restaurant in Tel Aviv. "My mother used to assemble it on Friday night and let it bake very slowly until Saturday morning. Then we would pull it out of the oven, warm and flaky, and serve it with tahini, hard-boiled eggs, and potatoes."

Sfikha is very easy to make (assuming you're using prepared puff pastry), and the secret to success is the quality of its ingredients. Tamarind pulp or pomegranate molasses is a must. Both impart a sweet-and-sour note that complements the rest of the ingredients and makes sfikha the unique treat that it is.

Makes about 20 pastries

1 tablespoon olive oil

1 onion, finely chopped

1 pound (½ kg) ground beef (preferably from short ribs)

1 heaping spoonful tamarind pulp or pomegranate syrup (pomegranate molasses)

Salt and freshly ground black pepper

About 1 pound (500 g) nondairy puff pastry, thawed overnight in the fridge

1 egg, beaten

1. Heat the olive oil in a skillet over medium heat. Add the onion and sauté until soft and translucent, about 5 minutes. Transfer to a bowl and let cool.

2. Add the ground beef to the bowl and season with the tamarind, salt, and pepper, and knead well with your hands. Form balls the size of golf balls and refrigerate until ready to use.

3. Preheat the oven to 430°F (220°C). Line a baking sheet with parchment.

4. Spread the puff pastry on a floured work surface and cut into squares of about 2 inches (5 cm). Brush with the egg and transfer to the baking sheet.

5. Place a meatball in the center of each pastry square. Flatten it slightly.

6. Bake for 20 minutes, or until golden. Serve warm or at room temperature.

SFIKHA SHABBAT BRUNCH Prepare tahini spread (see page 159); hard-boiled eggs (I like them a little bit underdone, with the yolk very soft); boiled and sliced potatoes, drizzled with olive oil and sprinkled with chopped chives or scallions; and a plate of vegetable crudités, such as radishes, kohlrabi, carrots, and celery. Arrange everything on a table, buffet style, and serve with oven-fresh sfikha pastries.

CHUKOR | Phyllo Spinach and Cheese Pastries

SEPHARDIC, TURKISH

Made with phyllo dough or puff pastry in individual-size pastries or in one large pie to share—either way a chukor is always shaped like a snail. My favorite is one made with cheese and spinach cloaked in flaky phyllo. Note that the spinach is added raw. The oven provides just enough heat to give it a nice texture while retaining its fresh flavor.

Makes 12 pastries

For the filling

1 pound (½ kg) fresh spinach leaves, trimmed and roughly chopped

9 ounces (250 g) feta cheese, crumbled

Pinch of ground nutmeg

Small pinch of salt

Freshly ground black pepper

2½ ounces (70 g) kashkaval, kasseri, or aged provolone cheese, grated

For the pastry

12 to 15 sheets phyllo dough, thawed overnight in the refrigerator

¼ cup olive oil or 4 tablespoons unsalted butter, melted, for brushing

Black and/or white sesame seeds

I. **Prepare the filling** Combine the spinach, feta, nutmeg, salt, pepper, and grated cheese in a large bowl. Go very light on the salt, because the cheeses are salty enough. Stir with a wooden spoon until well mixed.

2. Preheat the oven to 350°F (180°C). Line a baking sheet with parchment.

3. **Prepare the pastry** Remove the phyllo sheets from the refrigerator and cover with a damp kitchen towel. Leave them covered at all times to prevent drying. Brush 1 phyllo sheet with olive oil and place another sheet on top and brush it as well. Cut into 2 equal rectangles.

4. Place 3 to 4 tablespoons filling along the bottom part of the rectangle. Roll it into a log and shape the log into a spiral. Repeat with the remaining rectangles to make a total of 12 spirals.

5. Arrange on the baking sheet and brush with oil. Sprinkle with sesame seeds and bake for about 40 minutes, until golden brown. Serve warm.

Secrets of Phyllo

Working with prepared phyllo dough is easy. Just watch that it doesn't break or dry out.

1. Thaw it overnight in the refrigerator.
2. While working with one sheet, keep the rest covered with a damp towel at all times to prevent it from drying.
3. For the same reason, have all other ingredients for the recipe at hand and work quickly.

BANITZA | Phyllo and Cheese Pie

SEPHARDIC, BULGARIAN

Crispy on the outside and meltingly rich on the inside, this phyllo-and-cheese pastry is the star of Shavuot at the table of Bulgarian Jews. Turkish Jews prepare an almost identical pastry called börek, usually using yufka dough—a slightly thicker variety of phyllo. The latter can be found in Turkish groceries or online and yields a softer, juicier pie.

Makes one 11 x 7-inch (28 x 20-cm) pie

For the filling

4 eggs, beaten

1 cup heavy cream

½ cup milk

Freshly ground black pepper

9 ounces (250 g) crumbled feta cheese

9 ounces (250 g) coarsely grated kashkaval or Greek kasseri cheese (see below)

3½ ounces (100 g) grated Parmesan cheese

For the pastry

3½ tablespoons unsalted butter, melted

1 package (about 1 pound/500 g) phyllo dough, thawed overnight in the refrigerator

1. **Prepare the filling** Mix the eggs, cream, milk, pepper, feta, kashkaval, and Parmesan in a bowl.

2. Preheat the oven to 400°F (200°C).

3. **Prepare the pastry** Brush an 11 x 7-inch (28 x 20-cm) baking pan with some butter. Working quickly so as not to dry out the phyllo, line the bottom and sides with 1 sheet of phyllo (let it hang over the edge). Brush with more of the melted butter. Top with another sheet of phyllo and brush with butter again. Wrinkle 5 sheets of phyllo and arrange in the pan on top of the buttered phyllo. Spread on half of the cheese filling. Repeat one more time (with 5 wrinkled sheets of phyllo and the remaining filling). Brush butter onto 2 sheets of phyllo and lay them on the top layer to cover. Tuck in the hanging edges.

4. Bake for about 40 minutes, until golden. If preparing the pie in advance, bake for 30 minutes, cover, and keep in the refrigerator. Heat for 5 minutes in a preheated 400°F (200°C) oven before serving.

VARIATION

BANITZA WITH SPINACH AND CHEESE Roughly chop 10 ounces (300 g) fresh spinach leaves and sauté in 2 tablespoons unsalted butter until wilted. Add to the cheeses and mix well. Proceed as directed in the recipe.

Kashkaval Cheese

Made from sheep's milk, with a piquant, slightly tart flavor, kashkaval is the favorite aged cheese in Balkan cuisines, where it is usually grated and incorporated into savory baking. Greek kasseri cheese is very similar in taste and texture. Both are available at Greek and Middle Eastern groceries. Kasseri is also available at cheese counters in some supermarkets. If you can't find it, use a mixture of one-third pecorino and two-thirds aged mozzarella cheese.

PUFF PASTRY CHEESE BOUREKAS

BULGARIAN

Cheese bourekas were my snack of choice when I served in the military in the early 1980s. I would buy a few small pies at a branch of the Sami Bourekas chain next to my base and munch on them in the bus on the way home, ending up with pastry flakes speckled all over my uniform. To be honest, those bourekas were quite mediocre—the pastry (margarine based) had a funny aftertaste and the cheese filling was bland, but I liked them anyway. Sami Bourekas went out of business years ago, but the chain and its founder, Itzhak Elcolombari, should be credited with transforming these flaky homey pies into a national symbol.

The Israeli food scene is unimaginable without bourekas—triangles, squares, or snails; filled with cheese, potatoes, mushrooms, spinach, eggplants, pumpkin . . . there are even pizza-flavored bourekas. But the archetypal ones are triangular puff pastry pockets filled with a savory cheese mixture. Making them is easy and the quality will be as good as the ingredients you use. Taste them fresh from the oven and you will be hooked.

Makes 25 bourekas

For the filling

9 ounces (250 g) ricotta or fresh farmer cheese

4 ounces (120 g) feta cheese, crumbled

1 egg yolk

3½ ounces (100 g) hard cheese, such as kashkaval, Greek kasseri, Parmesan, pecorino, or Gruyère, grated

For the pastry

1 package (1 pound/500 g) all-butter puff pastry, thawed overnight in the refrigerator

1 egg, diluted with 1 tablespoon water

Sesame seeds

1. Preheat the oven to 350°F (180°C). Line two large baking sheets with parchment.

2. Prepare the filling Combine the ricotta, feta, egg yolk, and grated cheese in a large bowl and mix with a whisk or a wooden spoon until smooth.

3. Prepare the pastry Unfold the pastry sheet on a lightly floured work surface and roll into a 12-inch (30-cm) square. Cut into 4-inch (10-cm) squares.

4. Place a scant tablespoon of the filling in the center of each square. Wet a finger and run it around the edges of the square. Fold the square diagonally to make a triangular pocket. Pinch the edges together. Repeat with the rest of the squares.

5. Arrange the bourekas on the baking sheets, brush with the diluted egg, and sprinkle with sesame seeds.

6. Bake for 30 minutes, or until deep golden. Serve warm. Bourekas are best fresh from the oven. If you want to save them for later, freeze them and heat in a preheated 350°F (180°C) oven (no need to thaw) for 35 to 40 minutes.

TIP

I like my bourekas with a lot of cheese, which causes them sometimes to leak through while baking. If you prefer them neater looking, use less filling—a heaping teaspoon per boureka. You can also stir 1 teaspoon cornstarch into the filling to make it less runny.

BOUREKAS SANDWICH Jerusalemites call this combo bourekas pinukim ("bourekas treat") and on café menus it is often listed as "bourekas breakfast": Open up a freshly baked boureka and stuff it with a couple tomato slices, sliced pickles, and a sliced hard-boiled egg. Season with freshly ground black pepper.

Shabbat State of Mind

Eilat, the Red Sea resort town on the southern tip of Israel; mid-July. Outside the air crackles with arid heat, while guests at one of the leading hotels queue for Saturday lunch in the blissfully air-conditioned dining room. There are salads, grilled chicken, fish, and other light dishes suitable for the season, but the star of the menu is cholent, a heavy concoction of meat, beans, potatoes, and stuffed intestines cooked for hours and hours in the oven. Obviously, eating cholent has nothing to do with the weather, but rather with the Shabbat state of mind.

Many dishes in this book are served for Shabbat meals. In this chapter, you will find those specifically developed by Jewish cooks all over the world to comply with strict Shabbat rules: no lighting of fire and no manual work. It is fascinating how these restrictions gave birth to some of the most interesting Jewish foods.

EXILES CHOLENT

ASHKENAZI, ISRAELI

There is an element of drama in making cholent. Most dishes you taste and season as you go, reducing or increasing the heat or adding liquids as needed. Cholent is different. You compose this elaborate casserole on Friday afternoon, let it simmer for a couple hours, and then send it to the oven or leave it on a hot plate until Saturday noon. The rest is out of your hands: Will the meat be tender enough? Will the casserole dry out, God forbid? Will flavors and textures marry? You can only hope and pray.

On Saturday morning the house is already swimming in warm aromas as friends and family gather for a late brunch, with cholent (or hamin, as we call it in Israel) its main attraction. Over the years, I have made cholent many times, using various recipes and with varying levels of success. The following version charmed me at our first encounter. It was created by the talented chef Omer Miller and first published in a book on Israeli food that I edited. The recipe is based on the classic Ashkenazi cholent, but borrows freely from other Shabbat casseroles—spices from the Moroccan sehina, scented rice inspired by the Iraqi t'bit; the addition of dates and date honey seems to be Omer's personal twist. That is why we decided to call it Hamin Kibbutz Galuyot—the "integration of the exiles cholent" or Exiles Cholent for short.

Note that the rice and the pearl barley cook in separate bags—the traditional method calls for cloth bags, but plastic oven bags (available at supermarkets) are more practical.

Serves at least 12

¼ cup olive oil

4½ pounds (about 2 kg) stewing beef, such as boneless short ribs or beef chuck, cut into large chunks

Salt and freshly ground black pepper

5 onions, sliced

2 heads garlic, halved crosswise

2 cups white beans, soaked overnight and drained

8 medium red or Yukon Gold potatoes, peeled

3 to 4 beef marrow bones, soaked in ice water for 2 hours

1 celery root (celeriac), roughly chopped

1 parsley root or parsnip, roughly chopped

8 carrots, halved

10 dates, pitted

1. Heat the olive oil in a very large ovenproof pot. Season the meat with salt and pepper. Working in batches, brown the meat on all sides over medium-high heat. Transfer to a plate.

2. Add the onions to the same pot, reduce the heat to medium, and sauté until deep golden brown, 10 to 15 minutes. Add the garlic and beans and return the meat to the pot. Add the potatoes, marrow bones, celery root, parsley root, carrots, and dates. Dilute the honey with 2 to 3 tablespoons of hot water and pour over. Season with 1 tablespoon salt, the baharat, cayenne, 1 tablespoon of the cumin, and 1 tablespoon of the paprika.

3. Mix the remaining 1 tablespoon cumin and 1 tablespoon paprika with 2 teaspoons salt in a small bowl. Mix 1 tablespoon of this spice mixture into the rice and transfer to an oven bag. Close the bag, poke a few small holes in it, and place inside the pot, against one of its inner walls. In another oven bag, combine the barley and another tablespoon of the spice mixture. Close the bag, poke a few small holes in it, and place it in the pot in similar fashion. Arrange the eggs more or less uniformly in the pot.

4. Pour in the chicken stock and bring to a boil. Reduce the heat to the minimum and simmer, partially covered, for 2 hours. Taste the liquid and adjust the seasonings.

3 to 4 tablespoons date honey (silan, see below) or 2 to 3 tablespoons regular honey

Coarse salt and freshly ground black pepper

2 tablespoons baharat spice mix (see page 150)

½ teaspoon cayenne pepper or to taste

2 tablespoons ground cumin

2 tablespoons sweet paprika

1 cup white rice

1 cup pearl barley

8 to 10 eggs, unshelled

About 2 quarts (2 L) chicken stock or water

5. Preheat the oven to 215°F (100°C).

6. Cover the pot with a tight-fitting lid and place in the oven to cook for at least 8 hours or overnight.

7. To serve, bring the pot to the table. Open the bags and let each diner compose his or her own plate.

VARIATIONS

- Replace half of the beef with 8 chicken drumsticks.
- Replace half of the potatoes with 3 sweet potatoes (peeled and halved).

Silan

Many biblical scholars contend that the "honey" in the famous expression "Land of Milk and Honey" refers to silan. Silan is a syrup made from dates, similar to bee honey, but thinner, darker, and with a subtle caramel taste. In biblical times, date molasses and grape molasses were the most common sweeteners. Nowadays, silan is prevalent in Jewish Iraqi cuisine, where it is prepared from scratch and used almost exclusively to make Passover haroset. Silan is commercially produced in Israel and throughout the Middle East. A vegan alternative to bee honey, it is gaining global popularity and is available at kosher stores and Middle Eastern groceries (see Mail Order Sources, page 203). When you buy, be sure to look for versions without added sugar. Silan enhances the flavor and color of slow-cooked dishes and can be added to recipes calling for honey, caramel, maple syrup, molasses, or any dark-colored syrup. If you can't find it, substitute regular honey, but slightly reduce the amount because honey is a bit sweeter than silan.

T'BIT | Stuffed Chicken and Rice Hamin with Honey and Spices

IRAQI

Made of beans, beef, and starchy vegetables, Shabbat casseroles are pretty heavy. Iraqi t'bit is different. It has all the comforting essence of a very slowly cooked pot roast, but because it is made with chicken and rice (rather than beef and beans), it is considerably lighter. Just imagine how delicious the chicken tastes after it spends the night in the oven wrapped in a blanket of fragrant rice. You can make it with a whole chicken or with chicken parts. Here are both versions to start you off.

Since the rice cooks for such a long time, this is a perfect recipe in which to use brown rice instead of white and make your Shabbat lunch more nutritious.

T'bit I (With Whole Chicken)

Serves 6

For the stuffing

2 cups long-grain white rice or parboiled brown rice (see below)

4 tomatoes, grated (see page 162)

1 large onion, grated

2 garlic cloves, minced (optional)

1 to 2 tablespoons baharat spice mix (see page 150)

2 tablespoons vegetable oil

1 heaping teaspoon dried mint

Salt and freshly ground black pepper

For the chicken

1 whole chicken (3 pounds/1½ kg)

2 tablespoons olive oil

2 cups chicken stock or water

I. Prepare the stuffing Mix together the rice, tomatoes, onion, garlic (if using), baharat, vegetable oil, mint, salt, and pepper.

2. Prepare the chicken Fill the chicken's cavity with one-quarter of the stuffing and secure it with toothpicks or a trussing needle and thread.

3. Heat the olive oil in a large ovenproof pot with a tight-fitting lid and brown the stuffed chicken on all sides, about 15 minutes.

4. Arrange the remaining stuffing around the chicken, so that the chicken is half buried in it. Pour the chicken stock over and bring to a boil. Cook for 10 minutes, until the liquid is absorbed by the rice.

5. Preheat the oven to 215°F (100°C).

6. Cover the pot with a tight-fitting lid and place in the oven to cook for at least 8 hours or overnight.

VARIATION

This doesn't comply with strict Shabbat rules, but if you want crisp chicken skin and brown crust on the rice, remove the lid and raise the oven temperature to 400°F (200°C) for 15 minutes before serving.

To Parboil Brown Rice

Parboiling improves the texture of brown rice and enables you to use it in any recipe that calls for white rice. To cook 3 cups brown rice, bring to a boil 6 to 7 cups water with 2 to 3 teaspoons salt. Add the rice and boil for about 15 minutes, stirring occasionally. Drain. Refrigerate if it will be more than a couple hours before you use it.

T'bit 2 (With Chicken Thighs)

Serves 8 to 10

For the stuffing

½ cup long-grain white rice or parboiled brown rice (see page 149)

1 large tomato, diced

4 chicken gizzards, cleaned and diced (optional, but recommended)

Salt and freshly ground black pepper

1 teaspoon sweet paprika

1 teaspoon baharat spice mix (see below)

3 tablespoons olive oil

For the chicken

12 chicken thighs

1 tablespoon honey

1 tablespoon sweet paprika

Salt and freshly ground black pepper

For the casserole

½ cup olive oil

3 onions, chopped

4 garlic cloves, minced

1 tablespoon sweet paprika

½ teaspoon hot paprika

1 tablespoon baharat spice mix

1 teaspoon salt

2 tablespoons tomato paste

3 cups long-grain white rice or parboiled brown rice (see page 149)

1. Prepare the stuffing Mix together the rice, tomato, gizzards (if using), salt, pepper, sweet paprika, baharat, and olive oil in a bowl.

2. Prepare the chicken Gently run your fingers between the skin and the meat of the chicken parts to separate them and create "pockets." Fill each pocket with 2 to 3 teaspoons of the stuffing. Be careful not to overstuff because the rice doubles in volume when cooked. Secure with toothpicks.

3. Lightly brush the chicken pieces with honey and sweet paprika. Season with salt and pepper.

4. Prepare the casserole Heat the olive oil in a large ovenproof pot with a tight-fitting lid over medium heat. Add the onions and sauté for 6 to 7 minutes, until golden. Add the garlic, sweet paprika, hot paprika, baharat, salt, and tomato paste. Pour in 4 cups water and bring to a boil.

5. Preheat the oven to 215°F (100°C).

6. Add the rice to the pot and bring the liquid to a boil. Reduce the heat and carefully arrange the chicken pieces so the stuffed side is facing up and they are partially buried in the rice. Return to a boil and simmer for 10 minutes.

7. Cover the pot with a tight-fitting lid and place in the oven to cook for at least 8 hours or overnight. Serve hot.

Homemade Baharat

Baharat spice mix is available at Middle Eastern grocery stores, specialty markets, and online. You can also make your own. Grinding whole spices is ideal, but preground ones are fine, too.

1 tablespoon ground cardamom

1 tablespoon freshly ground black pepper

1 tablespoon ground cinnamon

1 tablespoon ground ginger

1½ teaspoons ground allspice

1½ teaspoons ground nutmeg

Combine all the ingredients in a bowl and mix well. Keep in a cool, dark place in an airtight jar. Use for meatballs, stuffed vegetables, and meat-filled pastries.

VEGAN PEARL BARLEY AND SILAN HAMIN

ISRAELI

At *Al Hashulchan,* the food magazine I run, there is a lovely tradition: For the first lunch of the week, we share leftovers from our respective Shabbat meals. This is how I became acquainted with this dish, which was prepared by Koby Kehaty, an avid cook and the husband of Yael Kalev, the executive editor of the magazine. Relatively light and easy to prepare, this casserole has the deep flavors and golden brown color of the traditional cholent. If you cannot find silan (date honey; see page 147), use regular honey, but the color won't be quite the same, and the recipe won't be vegan.

Serves 6

2 tablespoons olive oil

2 large onions, coarsely chopped

½ teaspoon ground cinnamon

½ teaspoon ground cumin

1½ teaspoons sweet paprika

½ teaspoon hot paprika, or to taste

Salt and freshly ground black pepper

4 to 5 garlic cloves, finely chopped

5 medium potatoes, peeled and cut into wedges

1 large sweet potato, peeled and cut into 1-inch (2½-cm) cubes

2 medium carrots, cut into large chunks

2 tablespoons date honey (silan) or 1½ tablespoons regular honey

2 cups vegetable stock or water

2 cups pearl barley, rinsed

⅓ cup raisins or pitted and chopped prunes

1 head garlic, halved

1. Preheat the oven to 215°F (100°C).

2. Heat the olive oil in a large ovenproof pot with a tight-fitting lid over medium-low heat. Add the onions and sauté until golden brown, 7 to 8 minutes. Remove the pot from the heat. Add the cinnamon, cumin, sweet paprika, hot paprika, salt, pepper, and chopped garlic and mix thoroughly.

3. Return the pot to the heat. Add the potatoes, sweet potato, and carrots and sauté over medium-low heat for 3 minutes.

4. Mix the date honey and vegetable stock in a bowl.

5. Add the barley and raisins to the pot and sauté for 1 minute. Add the halved garlic head and pour over the stock mixture until it covers the contents of the casserole. If necessary, add more stock. Bring to a boil and let simmer for 10 minutes.

6. Cover with a tight-fitting lid and place in the oven. After 1 hour, check the pot and add more liquid, if necessary. Cook for at least 8 hours or overnight. Serve hot.

VARIATIONS

• If you are not making the casserole for Shabbat, you can cook it for 1 hour at 300°F (150°C) and for 2 more hours at 215°F (100°C).

• Substitute beer for half of the liquids.

HAMIN MACARONI | Chicken Noodle Hamin

SEPHARDIC, JERUSALEMITE

Delicious and visually stunning is this alternative to the familiar cholent. Kids will love the combination of chicken and noodles, and so will grown-ups. Don't remove the chicken skin—it is important for the flavor and color. The noodles, called macaroni in Israel, are considerably longer than their American counterparts. In fact, they look more like fat, hollow spaghetti. Thick spaghetti will do just fine.

Serves 4 to 6

1 pound (½ kg) thick spaghetti, bavette, or maccheroni

4 chicken legs, separated into thighs and drumsticks

Salt and freshly ground black pepper

2 tablespoons vegetable oil

2 onions, sliced

10 garlic cloves, unpeeled

4 Yukon Gold or red potatoes, peeled and cut into ½-inch (1½-cm)-thick slices

4 to 6 eggs, unshelled

½ cup chicken stock or water

½ teaspoon ground turmeric

½ teaspoon ground cinnamon

1. Cook the pasta in a pot with a large amount of salted boiling water for 2 minutes less than instructed on the package. Drain.

2. Season the chicken parts with salt and pepper. Heat the vegetable oil in a large ovenproof pot with a tight-fitting lid and brown the chicken on all sides over medium heat until the skin is crisp and golden, about 10 minutes. Remove the chicken from the pot and set aside.

3. Add the onions and garlic to the same pot and sauté over medium heat until golden brown, 7 to 8 minutes. Remove from the pot.

4. Add the potato slices, season with salt and pepper, and sauté for 5 minutes on both sides until golden brown. Arrange in a single layer on the bottom of the pot.

5. Arrange the pasta on top of the potatoes, then return the chicken parts, onions, and garlic to the pot. Arrange the whole eggs on top of the chicken.

6. Mix the chicken stock, turmeric, and cinnamon in a bowl and pour over all. Bring to a boil and simmer for 10 minutes.

7. Preheat the oven to 215°F (100°C).

8. Cover the pot with a tight-fitting lid and place in the oven to cook for at least 8 hours or overnight. Before serving, remove the lid, place a large serving plate over the pot, and in one decisive movement, flip over the contents of the pot onto the plate. Serve hot.

JERUSALEM SWEET AND SPICY NOODLE KUGEL

ASHKENAZI, JERUSALEMITE

When Ashkenazi Jews brought their traditional noodle kugel to Jerusalem sometime during the nineteenth century, it underwent a curious transformation. Influenced by their Sephardic neighbors, eastern European cooks started to add lots of black pepper, which interplayed nicely with the sweet caramelized noodles. It is possible to bake the kugel in a cake pan or a casserole, but a tall ovenproof pot produces kugel with an eye-catching shape and airier texture.

Serves 6 to 8

14 ounces (400 g) egg noodles (small, medium, or large are fine; or, for the most beautiful look, mix different sizes and shapes)

$\frac{1}{3}$ cup vegetable oil

$1\frac{1}{2}$ cups (300 g) sugar

4 eggs

1 tablespoon salt

1 tablespoon freshly ground black pepper, or to taste

1 teaspoon ground cinnamon (optional)

1. Cook the noodles in a pot with a large amount of salted boiling water according to the package instructions. If using different kinds of pasta, cook each kind separately. Take care not to overcook.

2. Heat the vegetable oil in a tall, nonstick, medium ovenproof pot. Add 1 cup of the sugar and melt until caramelized and golden brown (5 minutes over a medium heat will do it). Add the noodles and stir to coat. Remove from the heat, transfer to a bowl, and let cool.

3. In a separate bowl, beat the eggs with the remaining $\frac{1}{2}$ cup sugar, the salt, pepper, and cinnamon (if using) and pour over the noodles. Mix well.

4. Return the mixture to the pot. Without stirring, cook over low heat until the edges begin to brown, 15 minutes.

5. Meanwhile, preheat the oven to 300°F (150°C).

6. Transfer the pot to the oven and bake for 2 to 3 hours (or overnight at 215°F/100°C).

7. Cool slightly and flip onto a serving platter. Slice as you would a cake. Kugel can be served warm or at room temperature.

SABICH | Egg and Eggplant Shabbat Breakfast Sandwich

IRAQI

Much more than the (peculiar) sum of its parts, sabich has gained cult status in Israel, and for good reason. Ask any Israeli what sabich is and the answer will be: a pita sandwich with fried eggplant, hard-boiled eggs, and amba (a spicy mango relish). Only a few will add that it is based on the traditional Iraqi Shabbat breakfast. As with every other Shabbat meal, all the ingredients of sabich (meaning "morning" in Arabic) are cooked in advance and spread out on the table, waiting for the family members to return from the synagogue and assemble their own breakfast treat. Today, sabich sandwiches can be found even in espresso bars, served on a variety of trendy breads.

The secret ingredient that pulls the whole thing off is the rich tenderness of a fried eggplant. So sorry, folks, no substitutes here; the eggplants have to be fried. For the lightest results, though, get young eggplants (they should feel light for their size when you hold them), slice them lengthwise, spread the eggplant slices on a nonreactive baking sheet, and sprinkle with coarse salt. Let them sweat out their fluids for about 40 minutes, wipe them dry with paper towels, and proceed with the recipe.

Serves 6 to 8

Vegetable oil for frying

2 large eggplants, thinly sliced lengthwise into $\frac{1}{3}$-inch (1-cm) slices

Tahini spread (see page 159)

6 to 8 fluffy pita breads or other flat breads

6 hard-boiled eggs or huevos haminados (see below)

Fresh parsley sprigs

Amba (see below)

Recommended additional toppings

Tomato slices, cooked and sliced potatoes, sliced pickled cucumbers, hummus spread

1. Pour the vegetable oil to a depth of 1 inch ($2\frac{1}{2}$ cm) in a wide pan and heat. Add the eggplant slices in a single layer and fry (in batches) on both sides until deep golden brown. Place on paper towels to soak up the excess oil.

2. To make the sandwich, spread the tahini in a pita or on a flat bread. Add the sliced eggs, eggplants, parsley sprigs, and drizzle with amba.

AMBA (SPICY MANGO RELISH) Bright yellow, hot, and pungent, Jewish Iraqi amba may be hard to find outside of Israel. You can substitute North African harissa (page 7), Yemenite zhug (page 162), or another hot relish. Indian hot pickles, such as mango, lime, garlic, or mixed vegetables, are great here. Do not confuse them with Indian chutneys, which are too sweet for this dish.

HUEVOS HAMINADOS In Ladino, the name of the dish means "eggs from the hamin (cholent) pot." Long cooking renders the egg whites brown and gives the yolks a creamy texture. In Sephardic households, huevos haminados are served for Shabbat breakfast along with savory pastries (for example, Sfikha, page 137). They can also be cooked on their own, though the texture won't be quite the same:

Line a wide pot with a thick layer of onion skins (you'll need plenty). Hang a couple of tea bags inside the pot, arrange the eggs in one layer on the onion skins, and pour in hot water to cover. Season with salt and pepper (some also add balsamic vinegar and/or cinnamon), and cook, uncovered, for an hour over low heat. Use an old pot because the skins and the tea will color the metal.

To make marbled brown eggs, remove the eggs from the boiling water after 30 minutes. Place in a plastic bag and crack slightly using a meat pounder. Take the eggs out of the bag, return them to the pot, and cook for another 30 minutes: The colored liquid will seep through the cracks and create the marbled pattern on the surface of the eggs.

THE RIGHT BREAD Freshly baked lafa (Middle Eastern pocketless flat bread) or fluffy pitas are perfect vessels for the sabich. The problem is that they are hard to come by. The dry, brittle pocket breads sold as pitas at most stores won't do. You can find fresh fluffy pitas at Middle Eastern bakeries that take pride in their craft and at some Middle Eastern groceries. You can also substitute flat breads from other cuisines, such as Italian focaccia or Indian chapati.

One of the most delicious and practical options is wheat tortillas. Heat them on both sides on a dry skillet only until warm and pliable and top as directed in the recipe. Roll and serve immediately or wrap in a sheet of wax paper and cut diagonally in the middle before serving. Sabich wraps travel well and are suitable for picnics or lunch on the go.

Tahini Spread

If you are not already familiar with this Middle Eastern classic, now is the time. Just pick the right kind of tahini paste (try to find imported Israeli brands like Prince, White Dove, or Al Arz—they taste the best) and you will discover an immensely versatile and healthy addition to so many dishes. In most cases, the first step would be making basic tahini spread—a procedure that takes less than a minute.

Combine ½ cup tahini (if the tahini in the jar has separated and there is oil on the top, shake the jar or stir it back in as you would do with peanut butter), the juice of ½ lemon, salt, and freshly ground black pepper. Using a whisk or a fork, gradually stir in ice-cold water. Don't be alarmed when the mixture becomes lumpy and thick (this is part of the process); keep adding water and whisking until the mixture turns smooth and creamy and the color changes from dark beige to ivory. If you plan to use it as a spread or a dip, leave it relatively thick (like mayonnaise). If you are making tahini dressing—for chopped salad or grilled vegetables or even meatballs—stir in more water.

As for additional seasoning, if the tahini is good quality, I don't think you need anything except salt, pepper, and lemon juice, but you can also add minced garlic and/or a dash of ground cumin.

KUBANEH | Yemenite Slow-Baked Shabbat Bread

YEMENI

The traditional diet of Yemenite Jews, one of the oldest Jewish communities in the world, is plain: a simple dish of legumes, a bowl of spicy soup with hilbe (a traditional dip made with fenugreek and considered a remedy for every imaginable disease), an occasional meat stew made with offals or other inexpensive cuts. What sets this ancient cuisine apart is its distinctive breads—from crumpetlike Lakhoukh (page 133) to kubaneh, arguably the most stunning of Yemenite breads. Butter-laced and leavened with fresh yeast, it is baked overnight in a Shabbat oven. The result has a deep mahogany-brown color, a delicately sweet taste, and a slightly crumbly texture.

Kubaneh is the centerpiece of the Yemenite Shabbat breakfast, which also includes hard-boiled eggs, zhug, and freshly grated tomatoes that cut through the fattiness of the butter. Though many modern cooks use margarine (which makes their kubaneh pareve), butter is better (clarified butter, even more so). To make kubaneh, you will need a medium ovenproof pot with tall straight sides. It does not have to be thick or heavy.

Serves 6 to 8

3½ cups (1 pound 2 ounces/500 g) unbleached all-purpose flour

¼ cup (2 ounces/50 g) sugar

1½ teaspoons instant yeast

1½ cups (12½ fluid ounces/360 ml) water

½ teaspoon salt

Vegetable oil for the pot and work surface

11 tablespoons (5½ ounces/150 g) very soft butter (preferably clarified; you can use high-quality ghee, which is Indian clarified butter)

To serve

Hard-boiled eggs or huevos haminados (see page 158)

Freshly grated tomatoes (see page 162)

Zhug (page 162) or other spicy sauce, such as harissa (page 7) or Tabasco

1. In the bowl of a stand mixer fitted with the dough hook, mix the flour, sugar, and yeast. Add the water gradually while kneading the mixture on low speed. Add the salt, increase the speed to medium, and knead for about 12 minutes, until the dough is smooth and elastic. If the dough is too stiff, add a little bit of water. Remove the bowl from the mixer, cover with a damp towel, and let the dough rest for 45 to 60 minutes, until it doubles in volume.

2. Transfer the dough to an oiled work surface and pound it slightly. Divide it into 5 even balls.

3. Roll out a ball and stretch it with your hands to make it as thin as possible. Spread it with about 2 tablespoons (30 g) of butter and roll into a log, then roll it into a spiral (like a cinnamon roll). Spread the spiral with a little bit more butter. Repeat with the rest of the dough balls.

4. Oil the pot and arrange the spirals inside in a circle, like a flower. Let rise until the dough reaches the brim of the pot, another 30 minutes.

5. Preheat the oven to 215°F (100°C).

6. Bake for at least 6 hours, preferably overnight.

7. Serve warm with hard-boiled eggs, grated tomatoes, and zhug or other spicy condiment. Alternatively, you can just add a few drops of Tabasco to the grated tomatoes.

(continued)

Zhug | YEMENI

Yemeni cuisine wouldn't be worthy of its name without this fiery dip, made from chile peppers, cilantro, garlic, and spices. The grandmothers' method for making zhug is to crush the ingredients between two stones. A stone mortar and pestle are a very good, albeit time-consuming, alternative. And yes, you can pulse it in a food processor, as long as there are no Yemenite grandmas around.

Makes 1 cup

Cloves from 2 heads garlic

$\frac{1}{2}$ cup fresh whole or coarsely chopped hot red chile peppers

2 cups fresh cilantro, coarsely chopped

10 cardamom seeds taken from whole cardamom pods

10 cloves

1 tablespoon black peppercorns

1 tablespoon cumin seeds

1 tablespoon salt

Juice of $\frac{1}{2}$ lemon

1. In a mortar and pestle (or in a food processor), crush the garlic, chiles, and cilantro to a nearly smooth paste.

2. Lightly roast the cardamom, cloves, peppercorns, and cumin in a dry skillet until fragrant. When they cool down, grind the spices in a spice (or coffee) grinder or pulse in a food processor.

3. Mix the cilantro paste with the spice mixture and season with the salt. Transfer to a jar with a tight-fitting lid and pour the lemon juice on top to preserve the green color. Store in the refrigerator for up to 4 days or freeze.

Grated Tomatoes

Grated raw tomatoes are the unsung heroes of Israeli cuisine. Their uses span from a quick breakfast at the kibbutz communal table to spicy condiments adding fresh zing to heavy Shabbat dishes. Fat free and a cinch to make, this trick of a recipe is worth making when summer tomatoes are at their peak. To prepare, place a coarse grater with large holes over a bowl, slice about $\frac{1}{8}$ inch off the stem end of a tomato and grate the tomato, starting with the cut end. You will end up with juicy, skin-free pulp in the bowl and a sheet of tomato skin in your hand. Chop the skin and add it to other dishes, if you like, or just toss it. Serve the tomato pulp as is or season with salt, black pepper, a squeeze of lemon, chopped garlic, chopped chile peppers, or fresh herbs. Grated tomatoes are often served with zhug.

Cakes, Cookies, and Desserts

More than perhaps any other type of food, desserts are associated in our minds with holidays and special occasions. The apfel kuchen or honey cake on Rosh Hashanah, the flourless cookies we eat only on Passover: Sweets and memories come hand in hand and carry with them the scents of celebrations we wait all year to experience again. Jewish desserts the world over combine flavors in interesting ways: chocolate with cinnamon; walnuts with orange blossom; dates with cardamom; poppy seeds with . . . well, poppy seeds by themselves are interesting!

FLUDEN WITH WALNUTS, POPPY SEEDS, AND APPLES

ASHKENAZI, HUNGARIAN

Fluden first caught my attention when a friend, an Israeli expat living in London, announced on Facebook that Bubbe Bella's famous fluden had traveled in a tin box all the way from the town of Beth Shemesh near Jerusalem and landed safely in her Hampstead apartment. My friend attached a photograph of a delicious-looking roulade stuffed with nuts and cherry preserves. A few months later, another friend told me about the fluden her mother-in-law used to bake. "She passed away before I had a chance to learn how to make it," my friend lamented. Then she went on to describe a layered cake filled with grated apples, which sounded very similar to the apple cake my grandma Vera used to make (page 169).

Some time later I suggested that we feature apple fluden in the Rosh Hashanah issue of our magazine (since apples are associated with Jewish New Year's Eve), but Yonit Naftali, one of our food editors, reacted with shock: "Rosh Hashanah? No way! Fluden is for Purim, and is always filled with poppy seeds." She told us how her Hungarian-born mother would bake her legendary fluden on Purim, gift wrap it, and hand Yonit a list of friends and neighbors she should deliver it to.

This really sparked our curiosity, and as we went on researching this elusive cake, we uncovered more versions: with sweet cheese, with jam, with dried figs, and even with guava (the last one hailed from a Jewish Brazilian baker). It turned out that fluden has always been a special-occasion cake, but those occasions have ranged from Rosh Hashanah to Purim to bar mitzvahs to wedding receptions. Though the origin of the name *fluden* is the Latin *fladon,* meaning "flat," many versions of the cake are tall and layered, while others are shaped as a roulade.

Yonit was right. Eva Naftali, her mom, does bake an incredible fluden. Here it is in all its glory: three delicious fillings nestled between four layers of wine-soaked pastry ("Hungarian Purim requires that even cakes get drunk," explains Yonit).

The recipe calls for ground poppy seeds, which are hard to come by. You can either grind whole poppy seeds (a clean coffee grinder is the best tool for the task) or just use canned poppy seed filling, which will also save time (see the variation).

Makes one 10-inch (25-cm) square cake

For the dough

3½ cups (1 pound 2 ounces/500 g) unbleached all-purpose flour

1 tablespoon instant yeast

¾ cup (5 ounces/150 g) sugar

Dash of salt

1 pound 2 ounces (2¼ sticks; 9 ounces/250 g) chilled unsalted butter, diced

2 egg yolks

1. Prepare the dough Combine the flour, yeast, sugar, and salt in the bowl of a stand mixer fitted with the dough hook. Add the butter, egg yolks, lemon zest, lemon juice, and brandy and mix on medium speed until combined and the texture is crumbly (resembles wet sand). Gradually pour in the wine and continue mixing until the dough comes together. Divide into 4 equal parts, wrap each one in plastic wrap, and refrigerate for 2 hours.

2. Prepare the poppy seed filling Combine the poppy seeds, milk, sugar, and vanilla in a saucepan and bring to a boil, stirring constantly. Remove from the heat. The mixture should be smooth, thick, and spreadable. If it is too dry, stir in a tablespoon or two of milk. Let cool. *(continued)*

2 teaspoons freshly grated lemon zest

1 tablespoon fresh lemon juice

1 tablespoon brandy

¼ cup (2 fluid ounces/60 ml) dry white wine or fresh apple juice

For the poppy seed filling

7 ounces (200 g) ground poppy seeds

½ cup (4 fluid ounces/120 ml) milk

½ cup (3½ ounces/100 g) sugar

1 teaspoon pure vanilla extract

For the walnut filling

11 ounces (300 g) shelled walnuts

⅓ cup (3 fluid ounces/80 g) milk

¼ cup (2 ounces/50 g) sugar

For the apple filling

5 tart baking apples, such as Granny Smith, peeled and cored

3 tablespoons sugar

1 tablespoon ground cinnamon

For the glaze

2 tablespoons smooth apricot jam, diluted in 1 tablespoon hot water

3. **Prepare the walnut filling** Puree the walnuts, milk, and sugar in a food processor to a smooth, spreadable paste. Add a tablespoon or two of milk if it is too dry.

4. **Prepare the apple filling** Grate the apples on a coarse grater and squeeze out the juice.

5. Preheat the oven to 350°F (180°C). Grease a deep 10-inch (25-cm) square baking pan.

6. Punch down the dough and knead briefly on a well-floured work surface. Roll out 1 piece of the dough to a square the size of the baking pan. Line the pan with it. Set aside any dough scraps. Spread with poppy seed filling and smooth evenly with a spatula. Roll out the second piece of dough and place it on top of the poppy seed filling. Spread on the walnut filling and smooth with a spatula. Roll out the third piece of dough and place it on top of the walnut filling. Distribute the grated apples evenly. Combine the sugar and cinnamon and sprinkle the top with the mixture. Roll out the last piece of dough and place it on top of the apples.

7. Roll out the dough scraps to a thin sheet. Cut ribbons using a pizza cutter or sharp knife and arrange in a crisscross pattern on top of the cake. Brush with the diluted jam glaze.

8. Bake the cake for 45 minutes, or until deep golden. Remove from the oven and cool completely before cutting. The cake will keep for up to 4 days in a tightly covered container at room temperature.

VARIATION

Instead of preparing the poppy seed filling, use one 11-ounce can of Poppy Seed Cake Filling (try Love'n Bake brand). Stir in 1 tablespoon fresh lemon juice, mix, and spread on the cake as directed. The filling will be a bit sweeter than in the original recipe, but because the cake is not overly sweet, it will work fine.

VERA'S APFEL KUCHEN | Apple Cake

ASHKENAZI, GERMAN

After becoming acquainted with fluden cakes (page 167) I realized that the apple cake my grandmother used to make could qualify as one, but for me it will always remain Vera's apfel kuchen. When she baked it, our whole apartment swam in the scent of cinnamon and warm apples. I, however, could also smell trouble. When the cake was ready, Grandma would cut it into squares and divide them between two plates—a large one for the family and a smaller one for herself. She would then hide her plate on the top shelf of the cupboard. Our share of the cake would disappear fast enough. This is when I would start making trips to the cupboard—I'd climb on a chair to reach the top shelf, take just one little piece, and drag the chair back to cover my trail. Naturally, the depleted plate was discovered and I would be reprimanded for being selfish and inconsiderate. It took me years to find out that I had at least one cake-looting partner, my dad—the only difference being he didn't have to climb on a chair.

Makes one 17 x 12-inch (40 x 30-cm) cake

For the dough

2¼ teaspoons instant yeast

2 teaspoons sugar

¾ cup (6 fluid ounces/180 ml) lukewarm milk

2½ cups (12 ounces/340 g) unbleached all-purpose flour

1¾ sticks (7 ounces/200 g) unsalted butter, melted

For the apple filling

5 pounds (2½ kg) tart baking apples, such as Granny Smith, peeled and cored

1 cup (7 ounces/200 g) sugar

½ teaspoon ground cinnamon

1 tablespoon fresh lemon juice

1 egg white (optional)

For the glaze

1 egg yolk

1. **Prepare the dough** Mix the yeast, sugar, and milk in a bowl and let stand for a few minutes until the mixture starts to bubble.

2. Place the flour in the bowl of a stand mixer fitted with the dough hook, add the melted butter and yeast mixture, and knead for 5 to 6 minutes to a soft, shiny dough. Cover with plastic wrap and refrigerate for 2 hours.

3. Remove the dough from the refrigerator and knead briefly by hand. If it feels sticky, add a little bit of flour.

4. Preheat the oven to 350°F (180°C). Grease a 17 x 12-inch (40 x 30-cm) baking sheet.

5. Punch down the dough and knead briefly on a well-floured work surface. Divide the dough in half and roll one piece to a rectangle the size of the baking sheet. Line the pan with it.

6. **Prepare the apple filling** Grate the apples on a coarse grater and squeeze out the juice. Add the sugar, cinnamon, and lemon juice. Taste the apples and adjust the sweetness/acidity by adding sugar and/or lemon juice. To make the filling a little more stable, stir in the egg white (if using).

7. Evenly spread the filling on the dough.

8. Roll out the remaining dough to a rectangle the size of the baking sheet and place it on top of the filling.

9. **Prepare the glaze** Dilute the yolk with a little bit of water and brush the surface of the dough. Using a fork, make a crisscross pattern on the glaze.

10. Bake for 40 to 45 minutes, until the cake is golden brown. Cool and cut into squares. Hide well. The cake will keep up to 4 days in a tightly covered container at room temperature.

HONIG LEKACH | Honey-Flavored Sponge Cake

ASHKENAZI

Honey cakes are an absolute must on the Ashkenazi Rosh Hashanah table. The most common are moist, dense, spice-laced pound cakes, reminiscent of German Lebkuchen. They can be very good, but perhaps a tad too heavy and sweet for an after-dinner dessert. This cake is different: Its texture is light and the honey flavor subtle, nicely balanced with lemon and brandy. I love serving it with tart fruit preserves, especially orange marmalade, or with baked apples.

Makes one 10-inch (26-cm) cake

7 eggs, separated

2 tablespoons (1 fluid ounce/30 ml) vegetable oil

2 tablespoons (1 fluid ounce/30 ml) honey

1 tablespoon (½ fluid ounce/15 ml) cognac or good-quality brandy

3 tablespoons (1½ fluid ounces/ 45 ml) fresh lemon juice

1¼ cups (9 ounces/250 g) granulated sugar

1½ cups (6 ounces/210 g) unbleached all-purpose flour

Confectioners' sugar (optional)

1. Preheat the oven to 350°F (180°C). Grease a 10-inch (26-cm) springform pan and dust it with flour.

2. Combine the egg yolks, vegetable oil, honey, cognac, and lemon juice and beat with a hand whisk until smooth.

3. In the bowl of a stand mixer fitted with the whisk attachment, beat the egg whites and granulated sugar to soft peaks.

4. Fold the yolk mixture into the beaten egg whites and gradually fold in the flour.

5. Pour the batter into the springform pan and bake for 35 minutes, or until a toothpick inserted into the center comes out dry. Cool, remove from the pan, and dust with confectioners' sugar (if using).

SWEET CHEESE PIE

ASHKENAZI, RUSSIAN

The best-known Jewish cheesecake in America is New York–style cheesecake—cream cheese based and set on a graham cracker crust. Eastern European cheesecakes are a different story. They are prepared with either short or raised dough and the cheese filling is on the custardy side. The cheese used to make cakes of this genre is a slightly sour, fresh farmer cheese, like the Russian tvorog, German quark, or Amish farmer cheese. If you can't find any of these, use ricotta, but add some lemon juice to get a hint of tartness—and don't forget to whip it with a hand whisk for a creamy texture.

Makes one 14 x 10-inch (35 x 25-cm) cake

For the dough

3 cups (15 ounces/420 g) unbleached all-purpose flour

½ cup (3½ ounces/100 g) granulated sugar

1 teaspoon pure vanilla extract

¼ cup (2 fluid ounces/60 ml) heavy cream

¼ cup (2 fluid ounces/60 ml) milk

1 egg plus 1 egg yolk

1½ teaspoons instant yeast

1¾ sticks (7 ounces/200 g) unsalted butter, softened

For the cheese filling

3 eggs

⅔ cup (5 ounces/140 g) granulated sugar

1 pound 10 ounces (750 g) farmer cheese, quark, or ricotta cheese

One 3.4-ounce (96-g) box instant vanilla pudding mix

2 tablespoons cornstarch

2 tablespoons freshly grated lemon zest

2 tablespoons fresh lemon juice (if using ricotta)

1 teaspoon pure vanilla extract

3 to 4 tablespoons golden raisins (optional)

For the glaze and garnish

1 egg yolk

2 tablespoons milk

Confectioners' sugar (optional)

1. Prepare the dough Combine the flour, granulated sugar, vanilla, cream, milk, egg, egg yolk, yeast, and butter in the bowl of a stand mixer fitted with the dough hook. Knead for 8 minutes to a soft and malleable dough. Cover with plastic wrap and refrigerate for at least 2 hours or up to overnight.

2. Preheat the oven to 350°F (180°C).

3. Prepare the filling Mix the eggs, granulated sugar, cheese, pudding mix, cornstarch, lemon zest, lemon juice (if using), and vanilla in a bowl by hand to a smooth texture. Stir in the raisins.

4. Punch down the dough and knead briefly on a well-floured work surface. Pinch off about a quarter of the dough and set aside.

5. Roll out the rest of the dough to a thin rectangle (about ¼ inch/½ cm thick), slightly bigger than the baking sheet.

6. Line a 14 x 10-inch (35 x 25-cm) baking sheet with the dough. Spread on the cheese filling and smooth with a spatula.

7. Roll out the rest of the dough to a thin rectangle slightly smaller than the size of the baking sheet. Roll a lattice cutter over the dough and gently pull the dough so that the slits open and a lattice shape is shown. Carefully lay the lattice layer on top of the cheese filling. If you don't have a lattice cutter, cut the pastry sheet into ribbons using a pizza cutter or a sharp knife and arrange in a crisscross pattern on top of the cheese filling.

8. Prepare the glaze and garnish Dilute the egg yolk with the milk and brush the top of the cake.

9. Bake for 40 minutes, or until the pastry is golden and the cheese filling sets. Let cool to room temperature and then refrigerate for at least 2 hours before serving. Dust with confectioners' sugar (if using) and cut into squares. The cake will keep, covered, in the refrigerator for 2 to 3 days.

BONNIE'S JAM AND PECAN RUGELACH

ASHKENAZI, AMERICAN

These dainty crescent-shaped pastries are one of the most iconic Jewish delicacies. The fillings range from cocoa to marmalade to nuts and the pastry is either yeasted or short. The only constant is the shape that gave rugelach (or rogalach) their name: *rog* means "horn" in Russian and Polish. Of all the jam-filled rugelach I have ever tasted, Bonnie Stern's are the most memorable. Bonnie, a famous Canadian cookbook author and a friend, admits that she has been trying new recipes for rugelach, but this recipe still tops them all.

Makes about 50 rugelach

For the dough

2 cups (10 ounces/280 g) unbleached all-purpose flour

½ pound (2 sticks; 8 ounces/220 g) cold, unsalted butter, cut into chunks

1 cup (8 ounces/220 g) cold cream cheese, cut into chunks

For the filling

1 cup firmly packed dark brown sugar

½ cup finely chopped toasted pecans

1 teaspoon ground cinnamon

½ cup best-quality apricot jam, or more if necessary

For the glaze

1 egg, beaten

½ cup granulated or coarse sugar

1. Prepare the dough Combine the flour and butter in a food processor or in the bowl of a stand mixer fitted with the paddle attachment until crumbly. Add the cream cheese and process only until a ball of dough is formed. Be careful not to overprocess. Divide the dough into 4 balls and wrap in plastic wrap. Refrigerate for a few hours or up to overnight.

2. Preheat the oven to 350°F (180°C). Line two large baking sheets with parchment.

3. Prepare the filling Combine the brown sugar, pecans, and cinnamon in a small bowl. Set aside.

4. Roll out each ball to a 10-inch (25-cm) circle. Spread each with about 2 tablespoons jam and sprinkle with a quarter of the brown sugar mixture.

5. Cut each circle into 12 triangular wedges. Roll each triangle from the base to the tip. Place on a baking sheet, tip-side down.

6. Prepare the glaze Brush each rugelach with the egg and sprinkle with the granulated sugar.

7. Bake for 20 to 25 minutes, until browned and crusty. Store in an airtight container for up to 1 week or freeze.

CHOCOLATE-CINNAMON BABKA

ASHKENAZI

This classic eastern European cake has long been a legend among American Jews. It is just as popular in Israel, where it is called krantz (German for "crown"), the name given to it by German-Jewish bakers who immigrated to Palestine in the 1930s and became the founding fathers of the local pastry industry. The following version, created by an Israeli pastry maker named Michal Michaeli, is quite decadent, with butter-rich pastry and plenty of best-quality chocolate in the filling.

Makes 2 babkas in loaf pans or I large babka in an angel food/Bundt pan

For the dough

1½ teaspoons instant yeast

¾ cup plus 1 tablespoon (7 fluid ounces/200 ml) lukewarm water

⅓ cup plus 1 tablespoon (3 ounces/80 g) sugar

1 egg plus 1 egg yolk

3 cups (15 ounces/420 g) unbleached all-purpose flour

½ teaspoon salt

1 stick plus 1 tablespoon (4½ ounces/125 g) unsalted butter, softened and cut into cubes

For the chocolate-cinnamon filling

1 pound 2 ounces (500 g) high-quality dark chocolate, coarsely chopped

½ cup (3½ ounces/100 g) sugar

1 tablespoon ground cinnamon

¾ stick (3 ounces/90g) butter, softened and cut into cubes

For the glaze

1 egg

1 tablespoon heavy cream or milk

I. Prepare the dough Mix the yeast, water, and 1 tablespoon of the sugar in a bowl and set aside for 5 minutes.

2. Combine the yeast mixture with the remaining ⅓ cup sugar, the egg, and egg yolk in the bowl of a stand mixer fitted with the dough hook and blend for about 3 minutes. Add the flour and salt and knead until fully combined. While kneading, add the butter gradually, in three to four batches. Knead for 10 minutes after the last addition of butter, to a soft and slightly sticky dough.

3. Place the dough in a greased bowl, cover with plastic wrap, and refrigerate for 1 hour.

4. Meanwhile, prepare the filling Melt the chocolate, sugar, and cinnamon in a heatproof bowl set over a pot of boiling water (bain-marie) and mix thoroughly to a smooth paste. Remove from the heat, add the butter, and stir to a smooth mixture.

5. Preheat the oven to 350°F (180°C). Grease two loaf pans or an angel food/Bundt pan.

6. Divide the dough in half on a floured work surface. Roll out one half of the dough into a 10 x 15-inch (25 x 40-cm) rectangle. Spread a generous layer of filling over the dough and roll into a long log. Fold the log in half in the shape of a horseshoe, then twist into a coil. Repeat with the remaining dough. Place one log in each loaf pan (if using). If you are making the cake in an angel food or Bundt pan, don't fold the logs; just twist them around each other to make one long coil and place it in the pan.

7. Prepare the glaze Beat the egg with the cream and brush the top of the cake(s).

8. Bake for about 40 minutes, until well browned. Store for up to 2 days in an airtight container, or freeze. Thaw for 1 hour at room temperature, then heat for 5 to 7 minutes in a preheated 350°F (180°C) oven.

CHOCOLATE RUGELACH

ASHKENAZI

In Israel, rugelach are almost always made with yeasted dough and filled with cocoa powder or cinnamon. The very best variety is prepared with layered (laminated) yeasted dough, similar to that used for croissants and Danish pastries, which is hard to make at home. This version, prepared with regular yeasted dough, comes pretty close. Glazing with sugar syrup helps to keep the rugelach fresh for a few days.

Makes about 50 rugelach

For the dough

3½ cups (1 pound 2 ounces/500 g) unbleached all-purpose flour

½ cup (3½ ounces/100 g) sugar

1½ teaspoons instant yeast

⅔ cup plus 2 tablespoons (7 fluid ounces/200 ml) milk

1 teaspoon salt

1 egg plus 2 egg yolks

7 tablespoons (3½ ounces/100 g) unsalted butter, softened

For the filling

10 tablespoons (1¼ sticks; 5 ounces/150 g) unsalted butter, softened

½ cup (2½ ounces/70 g) Dutch-process cocoa powder

¾ cup (5½ ounces/150 g) sugar

1 teaspoon ground cinnamon

For the syrup

½ cup sugar

½ cup water

1. Prepare the dough Combine the flour, sugar, yeast, milk, salt, egg, and egg yolks in the bowl of a stand mixer fitted with the dough hook and knead for 7 minutes. Add the butter and knead for another 5 minutes, until the dough is shiny and malleable.

2. Cover the bowl with plastic wrap and let rise for 45 minutes, until doubled in volume.

3. Prepare the filling Combine the butter, cocoa powder, sugar, and cinnamon in a clean mixer bowl. Replace the dough hook with the paddle attachment and beat until creamy.

4. Roll out the dough to a thin rectangle about 16 x 19 inches (40 x 48 cm). Spread the filling over the entire dough.

5. Using a pizza cutter or a sharp knife, cut the dough lengthwise into two rectangles, then cut each rectangle crosswise into 12 smaller rectangles (there should be 24 rectangles). Cut each rectangle in half on the diagonal so there are 48 triangles.

6. Roll each triangle from the base to the tip. Place on a parchment-lined baking sheet, tip side down. Let the rugelach rise for 30 minutes, until doubled in volume.

7. Preheat the oven to 350°F (180°C).

8. Bake for 15 to 20 minutes, until the rugelach are evenly browned.

9. While the rugelach are in the oven, prepare the syrup Bring the sugar and water to a boil and simmer for 4 to 5 minutes.

10. While the rugelach are still warm, generously brush them with the hot sugar syrup and let cool. Store for up to 2 days in an airtight container or freeze. Thaw for 15 minutes on the counter and heat for 5 to 7 minutes in a preheated 350°F (180°C) oven.

BABA BI TAMR | Date-Filled Biscuits

IRAQI

These look like little sesame-speckled pita breads, but their modest appearance hides a fragrant pastry and a succulent date filling. Prepackaged chopped pitted dates, available at Middle Eastern and Indian groceries and at health food stores, are the most convenient to use. But if you cannot find them, use regular dates (luscious Medjool are the best), pit, and chop them coarsely. Don't worry if they turn mushy—a pasty texture is exactly what you are looking for.

Makes about 30 large cookies

For the dough

7 cups (2 pounds 2 ounces/1 kg) unbleached all-purpose flour

1 tablespoon instant yeast

1 cup (8½ fluid ounces/240 ml) lukewarm water

3 tablespoons (2 ounces/60 g) sugar

1 teaspoon ground cardamom

1¾ sticks (7 ounces/200 g) unsalted butter, softened

3 tablespoons (1½ fluid ounces/ 45 ml) vegetable oil

Pinch of salt

For the filling

3½ cups (1 pound 2 ounces/500 g) vacuum-sealed pitted and chopped dates or regular dates, pitted and coarsely chopped

½ stick (2 ounces/50 g) unsalted butter, melted

½ teaspoon ground cardamom

½ teaspoon ground cinnamon

For the topping

1 egg, lightly beaten

½ cup sesame seeds

1. Prepare the dough Combine the flour, yeast, water, sugar, and cardamom in the bowl of a stand mixer fitted with the dough hook and knead for 2 to 3 minutes. Add the butter, vegetable oil, and salt and knead for another 8 minutes to a soft and malleable dough.

2. Transfer the dough to an oiled bowl, cover with plastic wrap, and let rise for about 1 hour until doubled in volume.

3. Prepare the filling Mix the dates, butter, cardamom, and cinnamon in a bowl. Form 30 balls about 1½ inches (3 cm) in diameter. Set aside

4. Preheat the oven to 350°F (180°C). Line two baking sheets with parchment.

5. Pinch off pieces of the dough and form about 30 balls 2 inches (5 cm) in diameter. Using your thumb, create a crater in the center of each dough ball, insert the prepared date balls, and smooth over to close. Press gently between two sheets of parchment so the cookie looks like a fat little pita approximately 4 inches (10 cm) in diameter. Arrange the cookies on the baking sheets, spacing them evenly. Brush the tops with the egg and prick 3 or 4 times with a fork. Sprinkle with the sesame seeds.

6. Bake for 10 to 15 minutes, until golden. Cool and store in an airtight container for up to 3 days.

MA'AMOUL | *Walnut-Stuffed Cookies*

SEPHARDIC, MIDDLE EASTERN

The ma'amoul (aka menena) is arguably the most popular cookie in Sephardic and Middle Eastern cuisines. It can be filled with dates, pistachios, almonds, dried figs, or walnuts. Semolina is frequently added to the dough, giving it an interesting crumbly texture. The filling and the dough are typically scented with rose water or orange blossom water. The pastry is sometimes sweet, while the filling is unsweetened, or vice versa. Or, as in the following version, both are barely sweet, but the baked cookies are generously dusted with confectioners' sugar.

What gives ma'amoul its distinctive shape is the grooved pattern obtained by using a special ma'amoul tweezer, but the effect can be created with a fork as well. Another option is to use wooden cookie molds if you can find them.

Makes about 40 cookies

For the dough

¾ cup (6½ fluid ounces/180 ml) water

½ cup (4 fluid ounces/110 ml) vegetable oil

1 teaspoon pure vanilla extract

1 teaspoon rose water or orange blossom water

3½ cups (1 pound 2 ounces/500 g) unbleached all-purpose flour

1½ cups (6½ ounces/230 g) semolina (cream of wheat or cream of farina)

2 teaspoons baking powder

2 sticks plus 5 tablespoons (10½ ounces/300 g) unsalted butter, softened

For the filling

2 cups walnuts, coarsely chopped

1 teaspoon pure vanilla extract

3 tablespoons granulated sugar

1 teaspoon ground cinnamon

For dusting

1 cup confectioners' sugar

I. Prepare the dough Combine the water, vegetable oil, vanilla, and rose water in the bowl of a stand mixer fitted with the dough hook. Place the flour, semolina, baking powder, and butter on top and knead for 5 minutes to a soft and malleable dough. Cover the bowl in plastic wrap and refrigerate for 1 hour.

2. Preheat the oven to 340°F (170°C). Line two baking sheets with parchment.

3. Prepare the filling Combine the walnuts, vanilla, granulated sugar, and cinnamon in a bowl.

4. Pinch off small pieces of the dough and roll them into balls the size of a walnut. Using your index finger, press gently to form a crater in the dough and turn your finger to enlarge the crater (be careful not to tear the dough). Fill with a teaspoon of the filling. Pinch the dough together over the filling, smooth it over and reshape into a ball. Create a grooved pattern using a fork or a ma'amoul tweezer. Place on a baking sheet and continue with the rest of the cookies.

5. Bake for 20 minutes. Take care not to overbake: Check the bottom of one cookie. If it is pale golden, the ma'amoul is ready. The top should remain light beige. Cool and dust very generously with confectioners' sugar. Store in an airtight container for up to 1 week.

VARIATION

Substitute the same amount of coarsely chopped pistachio nuts, or a combination of pistachios and walnuts, for the walnuts.

MAROCHINOS | Flourless Double Almond Cookies

SEPHARDIC

These easy-to-make macaroonlike treats are prepared with ground almonds and marzipan, which gives them a bold almond flavor and a slightly chewy texture. As they contain no flour, marochinos are perfect for Passover. The recipe yields a lot of cookies, but don't worry, they will be gone soon enough.

Makes about 100 small cookies

10½ ounces (300 g) plain best-quality marzipan

4 egg whites

2⅓ cups (3½ ounces/200 g) finely ground almonds (store-bought)

1¼ cups (5½ ounces/150 g) confectioners' sugar

Zest of 1 orange

1. Combine the marzipan and egg whites in the bowl of a stand mixer fitted with the paddle attachment and mix on medium speed until smooth.

2. Mix the ground almonds and confectioners' sugar in a bowl. Reduce the speed of the mixer, add the almond mixture, and process until the dough is smooth. Add the orange zest and mix until combined. Transfer to a pastry bag.

3. Preheat the oven to 250°F (120°C). Line two baking sheets with parchment.

4. Pipe cookies that are 1 inch (2½ cm) in diameter (or larger if you like) onto the baking sheets.

5. Bake for about 25 minutes, until firm and slightly dry to the touch. Cool and store in an airtight container for up to 1 week.

VARIATIONS

Replace the orange zest with a few drops of orange blossom water or 1 teaspoon ground cinnamon or ½ teaspoon ground cardamom.

SZILVÁS GOMBÓC | Plum Dumplings

HUNGARIAN

How can you tell real Hungarians? By the longing spark in their eyes when the word *gombóc* comes up. These potato dumplings, coated in buttery, golden bread crumbs, burst when bitten into, oozing hot, sweet plum juice. Authentic gombóc are prepared only with fresh plums (look for small round ones), but in the off-season plum jam may be used (see the variation). Another important point: Once the dumplings are formed, they must be cooked immediately. Otherwise, the texture will suffer.

Makes 15 to 18 large dumplings

For the filling

As many sugar cubes as there are plums

Ground cinnamon

2 pounds (1 kg) small or medium round plums, halved and pitted with a paring knife

For the dough

2 pounds (1 kg) red potatoes in their skins

1¾ cups (9 ounces/250 g) unbleached all-purpose flour

1 tablespoon semolina (cream of wheat or cream of farina)

1 tablespoon vegetable oil

1 egg

Salt

To coat and serve

4 tablespoons unsalted butter

1½ cups good-quality bread crumbs

Confectioners' sugar

Sour cream

1. Fill the plums Place a sugar cube and a little cinnamon in the pit cavity of half a plum, and top with another half to create a "whole" plum. Repeat with all the plums and sugar cubes.

2. Prepare the dough Boil the potatoes in their skins in a large saucepan until a fork penetrates smoothly. Remove from the pan and drain in a colander. When they're cool enough to handle, peel, then push the potatoes through a ricer or mash them with a potato masher, making sure no lumps remain (don't use a food processor, which will turn the potatoes into glue). Add the flour, semolina, vegetable oil, egg, and salt and knead gently with your hands to form a soft dough. Add a little flour if the dough is sticky.

3. Bring a large wide pot of lightly salted water to a boil.

4. Roll out the dough on a well-floured work surface to a ⅓-inch (1-cm)-thick rectangle. Cut into 3-inch (7-cm) squares (or smaller, depending on the size of the plums) and place a stuffed plum in the center of each rectangle. Wrap the edges of the dough around the plum and smooth it into a ball.

5. Slide the balls into the rapidly boiling water, working in batches, and cook for about 5 minutes, until they float. Turn gently and cook for another 2 to 3 minutes. Remove carefully with a slotted spoon to a large plate.

6. Coat and serve Meanwhile, melt the butter in a large skillet and toast the bread crumbs. Transfer the cooked dumplings to the pan and shake gently until the crumbs stick to the dumplings, 1 to 2 minutes. Serve immediately with confectioners' sugar and/or sour cream.

VARIATIONS

• Instead of plums, fill the dumplings with a spoonful of good-quality tart plum jam, store-bought or homemade.

• The dish can also be made with fresh apricots (look for small, firm ones), in which case it is usually known by its Austrian name: Marillenknödel.

AND RAISIN STRUDEL

ASHKENAZI, AUSTRO-HUNGARIAN

Old-school bakers still make paper-thin strudel dough from scratch, but store-bought phyllo brushed with butter yields excellent results. In this version, the apples are not precooked so they retain their fresh taste and a lot of bite. I find it charming, but if you prefer a softer, juicier filling, see the variation.

Makes 2 strudels

For the filling

3 pounds 5 ounces (1½ kg) tart baking apples, such as Granny Smith, peeled, cored, halved, and sliced

1 cup less 2 tablespoons (6 ounces/170 g) granulated sugar

4 ounces (110 g) hazelnuts or walnuts, roasted and coarsely ground

3½ ounces (100 g) dark or golden raisins

1 teaspoon ground cinnamon

Zest of ½ lemon

For the strudels

10 sheets frozen phyllo dough (preferably thick ones), thawed overnight in the refrigerator

1¾ sticks (7 ounces/200 g) unsalted butter, melted

¼ cup good-quality bread crumbs, mixed with 2 tablespoons granulated sugar

To serve

Confectioners' sugar

1. Preheat the oven to 400°F (200°C). Line a baking sheet with parchment.

2. **Prepare the filling** Mix the apples, granulated sugar, hazelnuts, raisins, cinnamon, and lemon zest in a large bowl.

3. **Prepare the strudels** Place one phyllo sheet on a work surface (cover the remaining sheets with a damp towel to prevent them from drying up). Brush with some of the melted butter and sprinkle with some of the bread crumb mixture. Place another sheet of phyllo dough on top, brush with butter, and sprinkle with bread crumbs. Repeat three more times, so that five sheets are layered.

4. Spoon half of the apple filling along the long side of the phyllo stack and roll the stack into a loose log. Transfer to the prepared baking sheet, seam-side down.

5. Repeat with the remaining phyllo dough, butter, bread crumbs, and filling.

6. Bake for 22 to 25 minutes, until golden. Remove from the oven, spread with the remaining melted butter, and cool slightly.

7. Dust with the confectioners' sugar and serve warm or at room temperature within a few hours. Goes great with crème fraîche or vanilla ice cream.

TIP

Phyllo dough turns very flaky and hard to slice when baked. The solution is to partially slice the strudel before it goes into the oven. With a sharp knife, mark the slices on top of the strudels. Cut through the top layer of phyllo but be careful not to cut all the way through. Bake, let cool, and then cut all the way through. Dust with confectioners' sugar.

VARIATION

STRUDEL WITH SAUTÉED APPLE FILLING Start by preparing the filling: Instead of slicing the apples, cut them into wedges. Melt 3 tablespoons unsalted butter in a sauté pan. Add granulated sugar and the apples and sauté over medium heat for 4 to 5 minutes. Mix ¼ cup fresh lemon juice with 2 tablespoons cornstarch and stir into the apples. Add the hazelnuts, raisins, cinnamon, and lemon zest and cook for another minute. Cool completely. Meanwhile, prepare the phyllo stacks. Fill and bake as directed.

GHRAYBEH | Orange Blossom Butter Cookies

SEPHARDIC, MIDDLE EASTERN

Eggless, light colored, and meltingly crumbly, this cookie is often compared with shortbread. What sets it apart from its Scottish counterpart is the orange blossom flavoring and its very subtle sweetness. Micky Shemo, a famous Israeli pastry chef who contributed a few of his favorite pastries to this collection, learned this recipe from his Turkish-born grandmother Mathilda. His version combines butter with oil and a touch of vanilla, which blends nicely with the orange blossom flavor.

Makes 40 to 45 cookies

1 stick plus 3 tablespoons (5 ounces/150 g) unsalted butter, softened

½ cup (100 g) granulated sugar

1 cup less 2 tablespoons (3½ ounces/100 g) confectioners' sugar

½ cup plus 2 tablespoons (5½ fluid ounces/150 ml) vegetable oil

½ teaspoon pure vanilla extract

2 tablespoons (1 fluid ounce/30 ml) water

1 teaspoon orange blossom water

3½ cups (1 pound 2 ounces/500 g) unbleached all-purpose flour

1 teaspoon baking powder

40 to 50 (about ½ cup) whole unpeeled almonds

1. Combine the butter, granulated sugar, confectioners' sugar, vegetable oil, and vanilla in the bowl of a stand mixer fitted with the paddle attachment and beat on medium speed for 2 minutes to a smooth paste. Add the water and orange blossom water and beat for a few more seconds.

2. Lower the speed and add the flour and baking powder, mixing only until the flour is incorporated and the texture is crumbly (and resembles wet sand).

3. Transfer the crumbs to a well-floured work surface and knead briefly to a smooth dough. Be careful not to overwork the dough—it might hurt the texture. Wrap in plastic wrap and refrigerate for 30 minutes.

4. Preheat the oven to 350F° (180°C). Line two baking sheets with parchment.

5. Pinch off pieces of dough the size of walnuts and roll them into balls. Arrange on the baking sheets, spacing them evenly. Insert an almond into the center of each cookie.

6. Bake for 20 minutes. The cookies will spread a little and change color to light beige. Chill completely before handling and store in an airtight container at room temperature for up to 10 days

SUTLACH (ARROZ CON LECHE) | Sweet Rice Pudding

SEPHARDIC, BALKAN

This dessert has two distinct versions: one made with rice flour (which is similar to cornstarch), the other with whole rice grains. Nir Dudek, who contributed this recipe, went for a middle way: He grinds the rice in the food processor to tiny flakes. The result is velvety yet with some al dente bite to it. It is customary to place the prepared pudding under a hot broiler for a few minutes for some beautiful scorch marks, like those on crème brûlée.

Serves 8

1¼ cups long-grain rice

5 cups milk

½ cup sugar

To serve

8 tablespoons orange marmalade or other tart fruit jam

Ground cinnamon

Roasted, unsalted shelled pistachio nuts (optional)

1. In a food processor, grind the rice with 1 cup of the milk to tiny flakes.

2. Put the mixture in a pan (preferably nonstick), along with the remaining 4 cups milk and the sugar. Bring to a boil, then reduce the heat and simmer for 25 to 30 minutes, stirring occasionally. Cook until the rice is soft and the pudding starts to thicken. It will still seem quite thin, but will thicken further when cooled. Put into a bowl and let cool.

3. Heat a broiler. Divide the sutlach among eight heatproof dessert bowls.

4. Heat under the broiler for 3 to 4 minutes, until nicely browned on top. Cool, cover with plastic wrap, and refrigerate. The pudding will keep 2 to 3 days in the fridge. Serve cold with a spoonful of jam, a sprinkling of cinnamon, and some pistachios (if using).

BASBOUSA | Juicy Semolina, Coconut, and Pistachio Cake

SEPHARDIC

When semolina cakes come out of the oven, they are not so sweet and are very crumbly, but once they are doused with hot and fragrant syrup, they turn moist and very sweet. The syrup also prevents them from drying out so they keep for a long time. The following version, from Ruth Oliver's kitchen, is the best I have ever tasted. Ground coconut and pistachio nuts add crunch, and cream renders the pastry richer.

Makes one 15 x 10-inch (40 x 25-cm) cake

For the cake

¾ cup (6½ fluid ounces/180 ml) vegetable oil

1½ cups (12 fluid ounces/350 ml) half-and-half (single cream)

1 cup (3½ ounces/100 g) shredded or flaked coconut

1 cup plus 2 tablespoons (5½ ounces/160 g) unbleached all-purpose flour

1¼ cups (9 ounces/250 g) semolina (cream of wheat or cream of farina)

½ cup (2 ounces/55 g) ground pistachio nuts

4 teaspoons baking powder

6 eggs

1½ cups (11 ounces/300 g) sugar

For the syrup

1½ cups water

1½ cups sugar

1 scant teaspoon ground cinnamon

1. Preheat the oven to 350°F (180°C).

2. Combine the vegetable oil and half-and-half in a large bowl.

3. Combine the coconut, flour, semolina, ground pistachios, and baking powder in a separate bowl. Stir into the oil mixture.

4. Beat the eggs and sugar in the bowl of a stand mixer fitted with the whisk attachment on high speed for 8 minutes until pale and fluffy. Gently fold the beaten eggs into the semolina batter.

5. Pour the batter into a deep rectangular baking pan approximately 15 x 10 inches (40 x 25 cm). Bake for 35 minutes, or until the cake turns golden and a toothpick inserted into the center comes out dry with a few crumbs adhering.

6. **While the cake is in the oven, prepare the syrup** Bring the water, sugar, and cinnamon to a boil in a small saucepan. Lower the heat and simmer for 15 minutes. Cool slightly.

7. Take the cake out of the oven and pour the syrup evenly over the warm cake. Cool completely and store in an airtight container for up to 1 week.

VARIATIONS

For a nondairy version, substitute the same amount of coconut milk for the half-and-half.

BASBOUSA DESSERT Cut the cake into small squares and top each square with a dollop of unsweetened whipped cream, crème fraîche, or thick yogurt. You may also add a spoonful of tart fruit preserves, or serve it with fruit compote (see page 196) or with wine-poached pears.

DRIED FRUIT, PEARS, AND WINE COMPOTE

ASHKENAZI, ISRAELI

H amekhaye," my grandfather Usher would sigh after gulping down a bowl of my grandmother's compote. When I was little, I was sure that *hamekhaye* was actually the name of the dish. This Yiddish expression (literally, "he who revives") is indeed fitting: What can be more refreshing than chilled compote at the end of a big meal? No less important, it is pareve and can be made ahead (perfect for Shabbat and holidays); it gets even better after spending a night in the fridge. True Ashkenazi compote is made with dried fruit, except during summer, when fresh fruits abound. This recipe, by Shaily Lipa, Israeli cookbook author and TV personality, fuses two classics—Jewish dried fruit compote and French pears poached in wine. The result is pretty and, indeed, reviving.

Serves 8

2 cups dry red wine

1 cup water

1 cup fresh orange juice

1 cup sugar

1 cinnamon stick, broken in half

2 cloves

12 prunes

12 dried apricots

8 small pears, peeled
(leave the stems on)

1. Combine the wine, water, orange juice, sugar, cinnamon, and cloves in a medium pan and bring to a boil. Add the prunes, dried apricots, and pears. Reduce the heat and simmer, uncovered, for 25 minutes, or until the pears are tender but still retain their shape.

2. Refrigerate in a covered bowl for at least 3 to 4 hours and up to 2 days. Serve chilled.

ASHUREH | Wheat Berries with Honey, Nuts, and Dried Fruits

SEPHARDIC, TURKISH

In Muslim tradition, ashureh (literally, "the tenth" in Arabic) is associated with a religious holiday that takes place on the tenth day of Muharram, the first month of the Islamic calendar. Turkish Jews borrowed the recipe from their Muslim neighbors and turned it into a special treat served at family gatherings celebrating a baby's first tooth (wheat berries resemble tiny baby teeth). Ashureh always contains grains, nuts, and dried fruits (and sometimes beans as well), but the texture ranges from porridgelike pudding to a kind of sweet cooked salad. Limor Laniado Tiroche, a private chef and food writer, went for the latter.

Serves 4 to 6

1 cup wheat berries, soaked in water for 3 to 8 hours and drained

4 cups water

5 tablespoons honey

1 teaspoon ground cinnamon

2 tablespoons unsalted butter

2 teaspoons rose water

5 dried apricots, chopped

2 to 3 dates, pitted and chopped

2 to 3 dried figs, chopped

5 prunes, pitted and chopped

25 almonds, chopped

25 walnuts, chopped

25 pistachio nuts, chopped

$\frac{1}{2}$ cup pomegranate seeds (optional)

1. Combine the wheat berries, water, honey, and cinnamon in a medium saucepan and bring to a boil. Reduce the heat and simmer, stirring occasionally, for about 1 hour to $1\frac{1}{2}$ hours (the exact time depends on how long the berries were soaked). At the end of the cooking, the berries should be very soft, slightly sticky, and a little liquid should remain at the bottom of the pan (like in cooking risotto). Add a little boiling water, if necessary.

2. Add the butter and rose water and stir well. Add the apricots, dates, figs, prunes, almonds, walnuts, and pistachios and cook for 5 more minutes on low heat unitl all the liquid is absorbed.

3. If desired, sprinkle on fresh pomegranate seeds and serve promptly.

MOFLETA | Sweet Pancake Stacks

MOROCCAN

Not to be confused with a muffuleta, the famous New Orleans sandwich, mofleta (or mufleta) is a Jewish Moroccan dessert prepared once a year during the festival of Mimouna. Celebrated immediately after Passover, Mimouna is a feast of hospitality and well wishes. Among its traditions is opening the house to neighbors and friends (even distant ones) and setting an extravagant table of treats—almost all of them sweet. Mofletas are the stars of the party—fried on the spot and served with honey and butter. The preparation is unusual, and as you will see, quite fun. Ruth Oliver once showed me how to do it, and in a matter of minutes I was flattening, frying, and flipping mofletas like a pro.

Makes about 40 pancakes

7 cups unbleached all-purpose flour

2 teaspoons instant yeast

1 tablespoon sugar

1 tablespoon salt

2½ to 3 cups water

1½ cups vegetable oil

Butter, for serving

Honey, for serving

1. Combine the flour, yeast, sugar, and salt in a mixing bowl and knead by hand, adding the water gradually, until a dough forms. The dough should be very soft but not sticky. Cover and let it stand for 15 minutes at room temperature.

2. Pour the vegetable oil into a small bowl.

3. Pinch off pieces of dough the size of an egg and form them into balls. Dip the balls into the oil and arrange on a baking sheet (the oil will prevent the dough from drying). Pour the remaining oil on the dough. Now the balls can wait for the guests to arrive (but no more than 1 hour).

4. Heat a 10- to 12-inch (25- to 30-cm) nonstick frying pan over medium heat. On a well-oiled work surface, using the palm of your hand, gently flatten one ball to a thin pancake 10 inches (25 cm) in diameter.

5. Place the pancake in the frying pan (no need to oil the pan, obviously) and fry for about 10 seconds until golden, and flip to the other side. Meanwhile, flatten a second pancake and place it on top of the first one. Wait for 30 seconds and flip both pancakes together, so that the new one is now at the bottom. Flatten the next pancake and put it on top of the first two, then flip all three. Continue until you have a stack of 12 to 15 pancakes. Serve at once with butter and honey on the side. Repeat making stacks with the remaining pancakes.

NUT AND DATE COINS

MOROCCAN

I f Mofleta (page 199) is sinfully rich, this sweetmeat, also associated with Mimouna celebrations, is almost a healthy choice by comparison. Yet another wonderful recipe from Micky Shemo.

Makes about 100 bite-size snacks

1 cup whole walnuts

1 cup whole pistachio nuts

1 cup whole almonds

1 cup whole pecans

1/3 cup honey

1/2 cup firmly packed light brown sugar

1 cup vacuum-sealed pitted and chopped dates or regular dates, pitted and chopped

1/2 teaspoon ground cinnamon

1/4 teaspoon ground cardamom

Pinch of salt

1 1/2 cups sesame seeds

1. Preheat the oven to 350°F (180°C). Line a baking sheet with parchment.

2. Put the walnuts, pistachios, almonds, and pecans on the baking sheet and roast for about 15 minutes. Cool slightly.

3. Meanwhile, bring the honey and brown sugar to a boil in a medium saucepan. Add the dates and mix until smooth. Remove from the heat.

4. Add to the pan the roasted nuts, cinnamon, cardamom, and salt and mix thoroughly. Refrigerate for 30 minutes.

5. Place the sesame seeds on a large plate.

6. Divide the nut and date mixture into 4 equal parts and roll each one into a log 1 1/2 inches (4 cm) in diameter.

7. Roll the logs in sesame, wrap in plastic wrap, and freeze for 1 hour. Slice into thin coins (about 1/4 inch/1/2 cm thick). The snacks will keep in the fridge for 3 to 4 days in an airtight container. To prolong their shelf life, keep the logs whole and slice the coins just before serving.

BIMUELOS | Honeyed Hanukkah Puffs

SEPHARDIC

Hanukkah celebrations call for foods fried in oil, and there are plenty of options in Jewish cuisines. Sephardic bimuelos—small, crispy, drizzled with cinnamon-scented honey syrup and garnished with walnuts—are among the easiest to make and the most delicious. This recipe was also contributed by Shaily Lipa.

Makes 40 puffs

For the dough

1 tablespoon instant yeast

¼ cup (2 ounces/60 g) sugar

2½ cups (20 fluid ounces/600 ml) lukewarm water

3½ cups (1 pound 2 ounces/500 g) unbleached all-purpose flour

2 eggs

1 teaspoon salt

Vegetable oil for deep-frying

For the syrup

¾ cup water

1 cup sugar

½ cup honey

1 large cinnamon stick, broken into 3 pieces

To serve

½ cup coarsely chopped walnuts

1. Prepare the dough Combine the yeast, sugar, and lukewarm water in a large mixing bowl and let stand for 10 minutes, until foamy.

2. Add the flour, eggs, and salt and whisk to a smooth, sticky dough. Cover with plastic wrap or a wet towel and let stand for about 1 hour, until doubled in volume.

3. Meanwhile, prepare the syrup Combine the water, sugar, honey, and cinnamon in a small saucepan and bring to a boil. Reduce the heat and simmer for 5 minutes, stirring frequently. Let cool.

4. Heat the vegetable oil for deep-frying in a large wide saucepan.

5. Pour some additional oil into a small bowl. Dip a tablespoon into the oil, take a spoonful of the dough, and slide the dough into the hot oil. Fry in batches, 6 to 7 puffs at a time, so as not to bring down the oil temperature, 2 to 3 minutes on each side. Using a slotted spoon, transfer to a paper towel–lined plate to absorb excess oil.

6. Arrange the warm puffs on a serving plate, drizzle with the syrup and sprinkle with the walnuts. Serve at once.

Mail Order Sources for Specialty Ingredients

Just a few years ago, you could only dream of finding "exotic" ingredients such as za'atar, silan, or kashkaval cheese in Main Street America. Nowadays, you can find them with little effort. Start your search for unfamiliar ingredients at the ethnic section of your supermarket, especially upscale groceries such as Whole Foods Market. If you live in or around a major city, there's a good chance you will find some there. Also check out your local ethnic groceries—Indian, Pakistani, Middle Eastern, Mediterranean, and even Russian—as many of them carry cross-cultural fare. You can also find almost everything online. The sources listed below ship across the continental United States and provide a large selection, high quality, good service, and reasonable prices.

Kalamala

A Middle Eastern grocery also featuring Persian, Kurdish, Armenian, Turkish, and Afghani delicacies. In the unlikely event you don't see what you're looking for, contact them and they will try to work with you.

www.kalamala.com

Tulumba

A Turkish grocery store featuring products from the Balkans, Turkey, the Mediterranean, and the Middle East. Also, if you by chance want to send flowers to Turkey, this is your place.

www.tulumba.com
866-885-8622

Kalustyan's

The landmark store for fine specialty international foods, featuring a very complete selection from many countries, with a focus on South Asian and Middle Eastern products. A pilgrimage destination for every foodie in New York, Kalustyan's also boasts jaw-dropping online offerings.

www.kalustyans.com
800-352-3451

Penzeys Spices

Really, any spice you can think of.

www.penzeys.com
800-741-7787

Acknowledgments

Ruth Oliver, a twentieth-generation Jerusalemite, is an amazing cook and cooking teacher, and one of the biggest-hearted people I have ever met. Ruth contributed many of her authentic recipes to this collection, generously shared with me her culinary wisdom, and prepared the dishes for the photo shoot.

Nirit Yadin, a kibbutznik and trained chef, has been living and teaching cooking in the United States for almost two decades. One of the most gifted food writers I have ever worked with, Nirit combines an intimate knowledge of Israeli and Jewish food with a keen understanding of the tastes and preferences of the American cook. Her unique perspective, revisions, and insights were instrumental in making this book accessible and useful to the American reader.

Amit Farber (designer and food stylist) and Daniel Lailah (photographer), my longtime friends and collaborators, truly captured the essence of this book. Their work brings to light the allure and relevance of Jewish food for the contemporary cook.

This book is the fruit of a transatlantic collaboration—me in Tel Aviv and the publishing team at Schocken Books in New York. Special thanks to my brilliant editor, Deborah Garrison, and to the Schocken team for their sensitivity, patience, and professionalism.

By its very nature this book is a group effort. So many chefs and home cooks shared their family recipes and stories with me. The names are too many to list here, but I credit everybody in the introductions to the recipes. I would like to take this opportunity to once again thank them all. They are the heart and the soul of this book; I just wrote down the recipes.

Index

(Page references in *italic* refer to illustrations.)

Shakshuka (Eggs Poached in Spicy Tomato Sauce), *102*, 103–4
Lime-Turmeric Broth, Chickpea and Chicken Dumplings in, 44, *45*
Lipa, Shaily, 196, 202
liver, chopped:
Erez's, 15
with Lots and Lots of Fried Onions, 12, *13*

M

Ma'amoul (Walnut-Stuffed Cookies), 182, *183*
Macaroni, Hamin (Chicken Noodle Hamin), *152*, 153
Mafroum (Meat and Potato "Sandwiches"), *74*, 75
mail order sources for specialty ingredients, 203
Mango Relish, Spicy, 158
Marochinos (Flourless Double Almond Cookies), *184*, 185
marzipan, in Flourless Double Almond Cookies, *184*, 185
Masala Beans, Green, 121
Mashawia (Fresh Tomatoes and Roasted Peppers Salsa), *10*, 11
Matboukha (Pepper and Tomato Slow-Cooked Salsa), 9
matzo:
Balls, 41
Herb and Meat Latkes, 22, *23*
meat:
Bourekas, Open-Face, *136*, 137
and Herb Latkes, 22, *23*
Kubbe with a Cheat, 52–3
Peppers Stuffed with Rice and, 69
and Potato "Sandwiches," *74*, 75
Spiced Minced, Potato Patties Stuffed with, 76, *77*
see also beef; braises; chicken; pot roasts; ragùs
meatballs:
Beef and Grilled Eggplant (Albondigas), 60, *61*
with Sour Cherries (Kebab Gerez), *62*, 63
Tart Potato and Celery Broth with (Batata Hamood), 50
with Tomatoes, Chickpeas, Swiss Chard, and Eggplants, 70
in Walnut and Pomegranate Sauce (Fesenjan), 64, 65

meatless mains, 101–21
Cabbage Rolls, Stuffed, with Sauerkraut (Töltött Káposzta), 71
Couscous with Vegetables (or Tuesday Couscous), 114, *115*
Eggs Poached in Spicy Tomato Sauce (Shakshuka), *102*, 103–4
Feta-Stuffed Pepper "Cutlets," 108, *109*
Green Masala Beans, 121
Mixed Vegetables Casserole (Türlü), 105
Pasta Casserole, "Before Shabbat," 120
Peppers Stuffed with Rice, 69
Rice Pilaf with Dried Apricots and Crispy Potato Crust (Tahdig), *116*, 117
Rice Pilaf with Lots and Lots of Fresh Herbs (Sabzi Polo), 110, *111*
Rice with Lentils (Mujaddara), *118*, 119
Spinach Flan, 106, *107*
Menena, or Ma'amoul (Walnut-Stuffed Cookies), 182, *183*
Messayir (Pickled Salad), 32
meze, *see* starters, salads, and noshes
Michaeli, Michal, 179
Middle Eastern cuisines, xii
flat breads, 159
Orange Blossom Butter Cookies (Ghraybeh), *190*, 191
Rice with Lentils (Mujaddara), *118*, 119
Tahini Spread, 159
Walnut-Stuffed Cookies (Ma'amoul), 182, *183*
see also Iraqi cuisine; Syrian (Aleppan) cuisine
Miller, Omer, 12, 146
Mimouna, dishes associated with:
Nut and Date Coins, *200*, 201
Pancake Stacks, Sweet (Mofleta), *198*, 199
Mini Cheese Buns (Bouikos con Kashkaval), 135
Mixed Stuffed Vegetables in Pomegranate Sauce, 72, *73*
Mixed Vegetables Casserole (Türlü), 105
Mofleta (Sweet Pancake Stacks), *198*, 199

Moroccan cuisine:
Beef Tagine with Dried Fruits and Nuts (Tanziye), 90, *91*
Beet Salad with Cumin and Cinnamon, 4, *5*
Carrot Salad, Spicy, 2, *3*
Chicken Tagine with Artichoke Hearts, *88*, 89
Fish Balls, Herbed, with Jerusalem Artichokes, Tomatoes, and Saffron, *66*, 67
Fish Ragù, Moroccan Spicy, *96*, 97
Lemons, Pickled, 2
Nut and Date Coins, *200*, 201
Orange and Black Olives Salad, *6*, 7
Pancake Stacks, Sweet (Mofleta), *198*, 199
paprika in, 98
Ras el Hanout Spice Mix, 51
Vegetables and Legume Soup, Spiced (H'rira), 51
see also North African cuisines
mozzarella, in Cheese and Egg–Filled Pies, 126, *127*
Mujaddara (Rice with Lentils), *118*, 119
Mushroom and Barley Soup, *38*, 39
Muslim cuisines, recipes with roots in:
Spiced Vegetables and Legume Soup (H'rira), 51
Wheat Berries with Honey, Nuts, and Dried Fruits (Ashureh), 197

N

Naftali, Yonit, 167
noodle(s):
"Before Shabbat" Pasta Casserole, 120
Chicken, Hamin, *152*, 153
Israeli Chicken Soup, 40
Kugel, Jerusalem Sweet and Spicy, 154, *155*
Norehlian, Rachel, 65
North African cuisines, xiv
Chicken Soup, Passover Green, *42*, 43
Couscous with Vegetables (or Tuesday Couscous), 114, *115*
Fish Stew, Two Ways, *96*, 97–8
Harissa, 7
Pepper and Tomato Slow-Cooked Salsa (Matboukha), 9

small dishes, *see* starters, salads, and noshes

sofrito:
  Beef and Potato, *80*, 81
  Chicken, 81

soups, 37–57
  adding lemon during cooking, 47
  Beet, Cabbage, and Beef (Borscht), 48, *49*
  Beet, with Kubbe, *54*, 55
  Chicken, Israeli, 40
  Chicken, Passover Green, *42*, 43
  Chickpea and Chicken Dumplings in Turmeric-Lime Broth (Gondi Nohodi), 44, *45*
  Hamood, with Rice, 50
  legume, reheating, 47
  Lentil Stew with Cumin, Garlic, and Coriander, 47
  Mushroom and Barley (Krupnik), *38*, 39
  Pumpkin, with Kubbe, *56*, 57
  Tart Potato and Celery Broth with Meatballs (Batata Hamood), 50
  Vegetables and Legume, Spiced (H'rira), 51

soups, dumplings for:
  Chickpea and Chicken, in Turmeric-Lime Broth (Gondi Nohodi), 44, *45*
  Gondalach, 46
  Matzo Balls (Kneidlach), 41
  Meat Kubbe with a Cheat, 52–3

spice mixes:
  Baharat, Homemade, 150
  Ras el Hanout, 51

Spicy Carrot Salad, 2, *3*
Spicy Fish Ragù, Moroccan, *96*, 97
Spicy Fish Ragù, Tunisian (Chreime), 98
Spicy Mango Relish (Amba), 158

spinach:
  Banitza with Cheese and, 140
  and Cheese Phyllo Pastries, *138*, 139
  Flan, 106, *107*
  Herb Frittata, 21
  Sponge Cake, Honey-Flavored (Honig Lekach), 170, *171*

spreads:
  Filfel Chuma, 104
  Herring-Apple Pâté (Forschmak), 31
  Pumpkin, Lemony (Chershi), 33
  Tahini, 159

squash, *see* butternut squash; pumpkin

starters, salads, and noshes, 1–34
  Beet and Herring Salad, Layered (Seliodka Pod Shuboy), 30
  Beet Salad with Cumin and Cinnamon, 4, *5*
  Carrot Salad, Spicy, 2, *3*
  Celeriac and Carrots in Lemon Sauce (Apio), 34, *35*
  Egg and Onion Salad (Zibale Mit Eyer), *16*, 17
  Eggplant Rolls with Walnut and Herb Filling (Badrijani Nigvzit), 20
  Eggplant Salad with Tomatoes and Onions (Blue Ones with Red Ones), 8
  Fish Cakes, Crispy, with Pine Nuts and Fresh Herbs, 26, 27
  Gefilte Fish, 24–5
  Herb and Meat Latkes (Ijeh B'lahmeh), 22, *23*
  Herb Frittata (Kuku Sabzi), 21
  Herring, Pickled, Homemade, 28, *29*
  Herring-Apple Pâté (Forschmak), 31
  Liver, Chopped, Erez's, 15
  Liver, Chopped, with Lots and Lots of Fried Onions (Gehakte Leber), 12, *13*
  Orange and Black Olives Salad, *6*, 7
  Pepper and Tomato Slow-Cooked Salsa (Matboukha), 9
  Pickled Salad (Messayir), 32
  Pumpkin Spread, Lemony (Chershi), 33
  Tomatoes, Fresh, and Roasted Peppers Salsa (Mashawia), *10*, 11

Stern, Bonnie, 82, 174

stews:
  Beef and Herb (Ghormeh Sabzi), 99
  Fish, North African, Two Ways, *96*, 97–8
  Lentil, with Cumin, Garlic, and Coriander, 47
  see also braises; casseroles

Stock, Fish, 24
Strudel, Apple and Raisin, 188, *189*
Stuffed Chicken and Rice Hamin with Honey and Spices (T'bit), *148*, 149–50

stuffed vegetables:
  Cabbage Rolls with Sauerkraut (Töltött Káposzta), 71

Meat and Potato "Sandwiches" (Mafroum), *74*, 75
Mixed, in Pomegranate Sauce, 72, *73*
Peppers Stuffed with Rice (Meatless Version), 69
Peppers Stuffed with Rice and Meat, 69
Potato Patties Stuffed with Spiced Minced Meat (Bistil), 76, *77*

Sunchokes (Jerusalem Artichokes), Herbed Fish Balls with Tomatoes, Saffron and, *66*, 67

Sutlach, or Arroz con Leche (Sweet Rice Pudding), 192, *193*

sweet-and-sour:
  Beef and Eggplant Casserole, 94
  Fish Casserole with Eggplant and Tomatoes, 92, *93*
  Sauce, Beef Tongue in, 95

sweet potatoes:
  Exiles Cholent, 147
  Lemony Pumpkin Spread, 33
  Vegan Pearl Barley and Silan Hamin, 151

Swiss Chard, Meatballs with Tomatoes, Chickpeas, Eggplants and, 70

Syrian (Aleppan) cuisine:
  Herb and Meat Latkes (Ijeh B'lahmeh), 22, *23*
  Lentil Stew with Cumin, Garlic, and Coriander, 47
  Meatballs with Sour Cherries (Kebab Gerez), *62*, 63
  Meat Bourekas, Open-Face (Sfikha), *136*, 137
  Mixed Stuffed Vegetables in Pomegranate Sauce, 72, *73*
  Rice with Lentils (Mujaddara), *118*, 119
  Tart Potato and Celery Broth with Meatballs (Batata Hamood), 50

Szilvás Gombóc (Plum Dumplings), 186, *187*

T

tagines:
  Beef, with Dried Fruits and Nuts (Tanziye), 90, *91*
  Chicken, with Artichoke Hearts, *88*, 89

A Note About the Author

The author of *The Book of New Israeli Food*, Janna Gur was born and raised in the former Soviet Union and immigrated to Israel in 1974. She is the founder and chief editor of *Al Hashulchan*, the leading Israeli food and wine magazine. She lives in Tel Aviv, on Israel's Mediterranean coast.

A Note About the Type

This book was set in Celeste, a typeface created in 1994 by the designer Chris Burke. He describes it as a modern, humanistic face having less contrast between thick and thin strokes than other modern types such as Bodoni, Didot, and Walbaum. Tempered by some old-style traits and with a contemporary, slightly modular letterspacing, Celeste is highly readable and especially adapted for current digital printing processes, which render an increasingly exacting letterform.

Composed by North Market Street Graphics,
Lancaster, Pennsylvania

Printed and bound by C&C Offset Printing Co., LTD,
Shenzhen, China

Designed by Cassandra J. Pappas